THE GREAT BIG COOKIE BOOK

THE GREAT BIG COOKIE BOOK

Over 200 recipes for cookies, brownies, scones, bars and biscuits

HILAIRE WALDEN

HERMES HOUSE

This edition is published by Hermes House, an imprint of Anness Publishing Ltd,
Blaby Road, Wigston, Leicestershire LE18 4SE

Email: info@anness.com

Web: www.hermeshouse.com; www.annesspublishing.com

If you like the images in this book and would like to investigate using them for publishing, promotions or advertising, please visit our website www.practicalpictures.com for more information.

Publisher: Joanna Lorenz
Project Editor: Joanne Rippin
Recipes supplied by: Liz Trigg, Patricia Lousada, Carla Capalbo, Laura Washburn, Frances Cleary, Norma MacMillan, Christine France, Pamela Westland, Hilaire Walden, Elizabeth Wolf-Cohen, Janice Murfitt, Carole Handslip, Steven Wheeler, Katherine Richmond, Joanna Farrow, Judy Williams, Sue Maggs, Carole Clements, Jacqueline Clark, Sarah Maxwell, Sallie Morris, Lesley Mackley, Roz Denny, Sarah Gates, Norma Miller, Maxine Clark, Shirley Gill, Judy Jackson, Gilly Love, Janet Brinkworth, Ruby Le Bois, Elisabeth Lambert Ortiz, Sohelia Kimberley
Photographers: Karl Adamson, Edward Allright, Steve Baxter, James Duncan, John Freeman, Michelle Garrett, Nelson Hargreaves, Amanda Heywood,David Jordan, Patrick McLeavey, Michael Michaels, Polly Wreford
Designer: Siân Keogh, Axis Design
Illustrator: Christos Chrysanthou, Axis Design

ETHICAL TRADING POLICY
At Anness Publishing we believe that business should be conducted in an ethical and ecologically sustainable way, with respect for the environment and a proper regard to the replacement of the natural resources we employ. As a publisher, we use a lot of wood pulp to make high-quality paper for printing, and that wood commonly comes from spruce trees. We are therefore currently growing more than 750,000 trees in three Scottish forest plantations: Berrymoss (130 hectares/320 acres), West Touxhill (125 hectares/305 acres) and Deveron Forest (75 hectares/185 acres). The forests we manage contain more than 3.5 times the number of trees employed each year in making paper for the books we manufacture. Because of this ongoing ecological investment programme, you, as our customer, can have the pleasure and reassurance of knowing that a tree is being cultivated on your behalf to naturally replace the materials used to make the book you are holding. Our forestry programme is run in accordance with the UK Woodland Assurance Scheme (UKWAS) and will be certified by the internationally recognized Forest Stewardship Council (FSC). For further information about this scheme, go to www.annesspublishing.com/trees

NOTES
For all recipes, quantities are given in both metric and imperial measures and, where appropriate, in standard cups and spoons.
Follow one set of measures, but not a mixture, because they are not interchangeable.
Standard spoon and cup measures are level. 1 tsp = 5ml, 1 tbsp = 15ml, 1 cup = 250ml/8fl oz.
Australian standard tablespoons are 20ml. Australian readers should use 3 tsp in place of 1 tbsp for measuring small quantities.
American pints are 16fl oz/2 cups. American readers should use 20fl oz/2.5 cups in place of 1 pint when measuring liquids.
Electric oven temperatures in this book are for conventional ovens. When using a fan oven, the temperature will probably need to be reduced by about 10–20°C/20–40°F. Since ovens vary, you should check with your manufacturer's instruction book for guidance.
Medium (US large) eggs are used unless otherwise stated.

Contents

Introduction

Americans call them cookies and the British traditionally use the term biscuits, although now the word cookie has become quite common all over the world.

Whichever name is used, cookies and biscuits are individual, small, crisp, baked sweet and savoury cakes that are good to nibble: the sweet ones with a cup of coffee or tea or other drink, or to serve with ice cream or other light dessert; the savoury ones with a drink or soup.

The American word 'cookie' is of Dutch origin, from the word *koekje* meaning little cake. The origins of the biscuit are to be found in the word itself: it comes from the French *bis cuit,* meaning twice cooked, and goes back to the days when bakers put slices of newly-baked bread back into the cooking oven, so that they dried out completely, becoming something like a rusk. This was really a method of preservation for it enabled the cookies to be kept for a long time; so long, in fact that they could be taken as a basic food item, known as 'ships' biscuits', on long sea voyages.

For many years housewives continued with the practice of drying their biscuits a second time, and it was not until the beginning of the last century that the habit died out. Then both the quality and variety of biscuits that could be made improved dramatically.

A batch of homemade cookies will fill your kitchen with a wonderful aroma when they are ready to come out of the oven. There is a great difference between homemade cookies and the commercial ones sold in shops and supermarkets. Packaged, mass-produced cookies are more concerned with profit and long shelf-life. They are usually too sweet, contain additives and their character and flavour, let alone purity, cannot compare with a tasty cookie from your own store cupboard. Baking your own cookies means you can use only the best ingredients.

There is almost no end to the range of cookies that can be made at home, using recipes that, over the years, have become great favourites the world over, with adults, teenagers and children alike. Many countries of the world have classic recipes and their own traditional favourites, such as Mexican Biscochitos.

This comprehensive collection of recipes suits every occasion and every taste, no matter if the fancy is for something rich and indulgent or traditionally wholesome, delightfully crisp or moist and chewy, satisfyingly chunky or elegantly thin, nutty or chocolatey. This book will inspire you to bake your favourite cookies for high days, holidays and special occasions, delight your friends to a gift-wrapped box of homemade goodies, keep some dough in the freezer for unexpected guests, and determine never again to resort to the supermarket for your cookies, brownies, bars or biscuits.

▶ *Cookies are not only ideal for everyday eating, or special treats at home; they can also be gift-wrapped and given away as a special gift.*

Cookie Tips and Techniques

Cookies can be made using a wide variety of methods to suit all ranges of ability, and to match the time and ingredients available. Most cookies are easy to make and special skills are rarely required. But, as with most things, once you know exactly the right way to do something, it becomes that much quicker, easier and enjoyable, and the results are far more likely to be successful. The following pages in the Cookie Tips & Techniques section provide all the information you will need to make successful cookies every time, with the minimum amount of effort.

You will find advice on choosing the most appropriate ingredients for the particular cookie you are making, and handy tips on how to carry out simple but vital tasks like measuring accurately. There are detailed instructions for all the methods used for making and shaping cookies, including piping the raw mixture, as well as the various methods of melting chocolate. Ideas for making cookies look really attractive are also included, and the way to make piping bags from greaseproof paper is described.

There are also recommendations on storing the made cookies so they will remain fresh for as long as possible, plus ideas on how to wrap and present your cookies so they become special gifts with a strong personal feel.

Store cupboard

The ingredients for cookie making can be found in most people's store cupboards and fridges.

Chocolate Buy good quality chocolate with at least 50% cocoa solids for baking. Plain chocolate gives a distinctive strong, rich flavour while milk chocolate has a sweeter taste. White chocolate often does not contain any cocoa solids, and lacks the flavour of true chocolate. It is the most difficult chocolate to melt and has poor setting qualities.

Dried fruits Today, most dried fruits are dried by artificial heat rather than by the sun, and are treated with sulphur dioxide to help their preservation. Oils are sometimes sprayed on to the fruit to give a shiny appearance and to prevent them sticking together. Try to buy fruit which have been coated with vegetable oils not mineral oils.

Eggs Eggs should be at room temperature so, if you keep them in the fridge, move the number you want to room temperature at least 30 minutes before making a recipe.

Butter and margarine Butter gives the best flavour to cookies and should be used whenever possible, especially when there is a high fat content, as in shortbread. However, it can be used interchangeably with hard block margarine. Butter or margarine to be used for creaming with sugar needs to be at room temperature and softened. For rubbing in, the fat should be at a cool room temperature, not fridge hard, and chopped quite finely.

Soft margarine is really only suitable for making cookies by the all-in-one method and when the fat has to be melted.

Flours Flour provides the structure that makes the cookies. Always sift flour. Not only will this remove any lumps, which are rare nowadays, but it also lightens the flour by incorporating air, and makes it easier to mix in.

Self-raising flour has raising agents added and is the type of flour most usually used in straightforward cookies that need to rise.

Plain flour is used when rising is considered a fault, as when making shortbread. Rich or heavy mixtures that should be raised also often call for plain flour plus additional raising agents in the specific proportions required for the particular recipe.

Wholemeal flour adds more flavour than white flour and is the healthier option but does produce denser cookies. When lightness is important extra raising agents should be added. Some recipes work well with a mixture of white and wholemeal flour.

Glacé fruits Wash glacé fruits before using them to remove the syrupy coating, then dry thoroughly.

Nuts Nuts become rancid if stored for too long, in the light or at too high a temperature, so only buy in amounts that you will use within 1-2 months and keep them in an airtight container in a cool, dark cupboard. Alternatively, freeze them for up to 1 year.

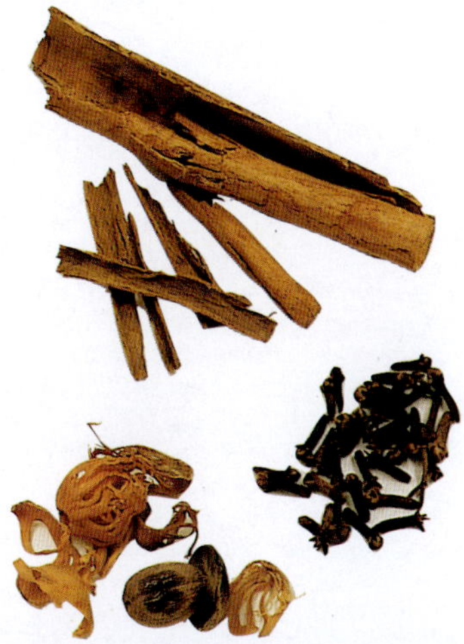

Spices Ground cinnamon, ginger, mixed spice, nutmeg and cloves may be used in cookies. All spices should be as fresh as possible. Buy in small quantities to use within a few months.

Honey Honey adds its own distinctive flavour to cookies. It contains 17% water so you will need to use slightly more honey than sugar, and reduce the amounts of the other liquids used. For easy mixing in, use clear honey.

Sugars Caster sugar is the best sweetener to use for the creaming method because the crystals dissolve easily and quickly when creamed with the fat. Granulated sugar is coarser textured than caster sugar so this is best used for rubbed-in mixtures and when the sugar is heated with the fat or liquid until it dissolves. Icing sugar appears in the ingredients for some cookie recipes where it is important that the sugar dissolves very readily. Demerara sugar can be used when the sugar is dissolved over heat before being added to the dry ingredients. Soft light and dark brown sugars are used when a richer flavour and colour are called for.

Equipment

A delightful aspect of cookie making is that it requires the minimum of special equipment.

You can make quite a range of cookies with just a mixing bowl, measures or weights, a wooden spoon, a baking sheet and a wire rack. Only a few items are needed to extend the range much further. Many supermarkets now sell all you will need for cookie making.

Baking tins Use good quality sturdy tins; thin, cheap tins will buckle with time. Cheap tins also heat more quickly so cookies are liable to cook quickly, brown and stick to them more readily. Non-stick tins, of course, save greasing, and lining when called for, greatly reduce sticking and cut down on washing up.

Cannelle knife This tool is great for carving stripes in the skin of citrus fruit. Pare off thin strips before slicing the fruit to make an attractive edge.

Cutters Cutters are available in many different shapes and sizes, ranging from simple plain biscuit circles in various sizes, to small cutters for *petits fours* and savoury cocktail nibbles, to animal shapes, hearts and flowers. For best results, the important criterion that applies to all cutters is that they should be sharp, to give a good clear, sharp outline. This really means that they should be made from metal; plastic cutters tend to compress the cut edges.

To use a cutter, press down firmly on the cutter so that it cuts straight down right through the dough. Then lift up the cutter, without twisting it.

If you want to cut out a shape for which you do not have a cutter, the thing to do is to make a template, or pattern. This is very easy.

Trace or draw the design on to greaseproof paper or card and cut it out using scissors. Lay the template on to the rolled out cookie dough. Use the point of a large, sharp knife to carefully cut around the template, taking care not to drag it. With a thin metal pallette knife or fish slice, transfer the shape to the prepared baking sheet, without distorting the shape.

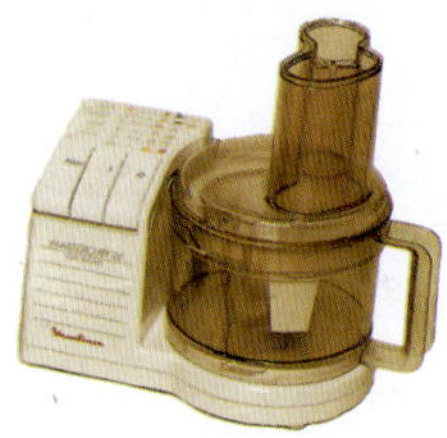

Food processor Although food processors save time, their drawback is their very speed; they work so fast that you must be careful not to overmix a mixture. Food processors combine rather than beat ingredients together, so they are not so useful for recipes where lightness is important. Also, many models cannot whisk egg whites, and even in those designed for whisking, the whites will not become really stiff.

Knives A round-bladed knife can be used for the initial stages of cutting in the fat before it is rubbed in. Large, sharp knives are needed for cutting cleanly and efficiently through rolled-out dough, or refrigerated dough. Palette knives are invaluable for spreading and smoothing mixtures in cake tins, transferring cut out cookies to baking sheets before baking and then transferring the baked cookies to a wire rack to cool. They can also be used for spreading icing on cookies.

Measures A set of accurate measuring spoons is vital for measuring 15ml/1 tablespoon, 5ml/1 teaspoon and fractions of teaspoons. All the amounts given in recipes are for level spoonfuls unless otherwise stated. For liquids, use a heatproof jug, preferably see-through, that is calibrated for both imperial and metric measures.

Pastry brushes A large pastry brush is very useful for brushing surplus flour from work surfaces and cookie doughs that are being rolled out, and for greasing cake tins. A pastry brush is also needed for brushing on glazes. Buy good quality brushes with firmly-fixed bristles.

Piping bags and nozzles A medium piping bag with a selection of nozzles is very useful to have for piping uncooked cookie dough, and for decorating cookies after baking. Use small disposable piping bags for chocolate or icing, where a fine line is required.

Rolling pin Rolling pins made of wood are the most common, but you can now buy marble or even plastic ones which are considered to be more hygienic.

Scales A good set of scales is essential for successful cookie making. Whether you use spring balance, modern electronic or old-fashioned balanced scales with a set of weights, test them frequently for accuracy by putting something on them which has the weight printed on it.

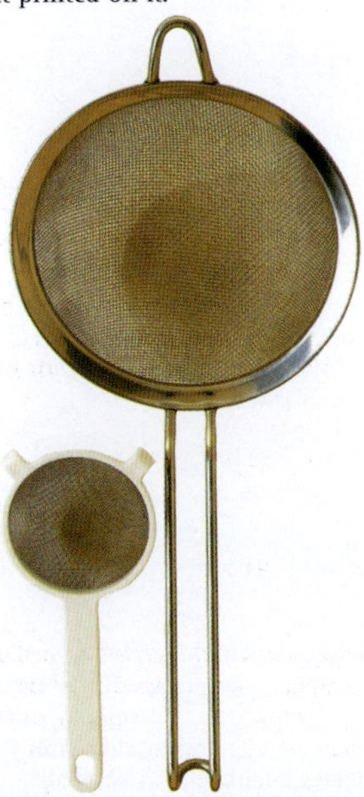

Sieves If possible have a set of strong sieves in 2 or 3 different sizes.

Skewers and cocktail sticks Either of these can be used for testing whether cookie mixtures are cooked.

Spatulas A flexible rubber spatula is indispensable for scraping every last morsel from the mixing bowl into the cake tin.

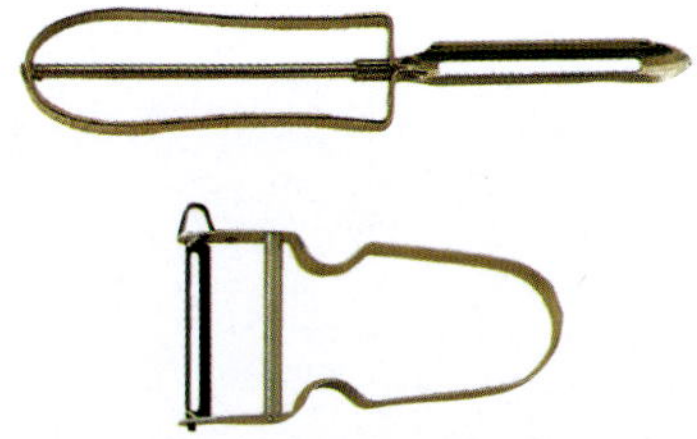

Swivel-blade peelers Both long-handled and broad-handled peelers are the best tools for peeling fruit.

Tea strainer A tea strainer will come in handy for sifting icing sugar over cookies as last-minute decoration.

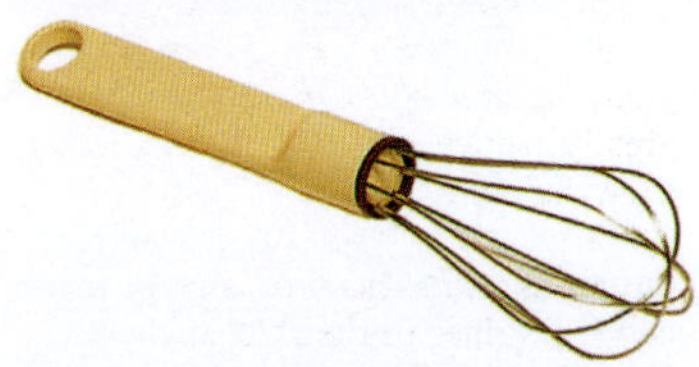

Whisk Use either a wire balloon whisk or a rotary whisk for beating eggs together. It is a good idea to have two sizes of balloon whisks, to suit the amount of mixture.

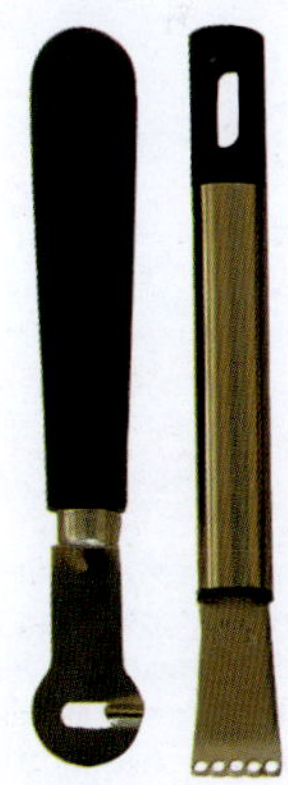

Zester Ideal for citrus fruit, a zester has the same function as a cannelle knife but produces a row of thin stripes.

Measuring ingredients

Cooks with years of experience may not need to measure ingredients, but if you are a beginner or are trying a new recipe for the first time, it is best to follow instructions carefully. Also, measuring ingredients precisely will ensure consistent results.

1 For liquids measured in pints or litres: use a glass or clear plastic measuring jug. Put it on a flat surface and pour in the liquid. Bend down and check that the liquid is level with the marking on the jug, as specified in the recipe.

2 For liquids measured in spoons: pour the liquid into the measuring spoon, to the brim, and then pour it into the mixing bowl. Do not hold the spoon over the bowl when measuring because some liquid may overflow.

3 For measuring dry ingredients in a spoon: fill the spoon, scooping up the ingredient. Level the surface with the rim of the spoon, using the straight edge of a knife.

4 For measuring dry ingredients by weight: scoop or pour on to the scales, watching the dial or reading carefully. Balance scales give more accurate readings than spring scales.

5 For measuring syrups: set the mixing bowl on the scales and turn the gauge to zero, or make a note of the weight. Pour in the required weight of syrup.

6 For measuring butter: cut with a sharp knife and weigh, or cut off the specified amount following the markings on the wrapping paper.

Making cookies by the rubbing in method

Plain cookies are usually made by rubbing the fat into the flour. For this, the fat, whether butter, margarine or lard, should be neither rock hard from the fridge, nor too warm. It is first chopped into small pieces, then added to the dry ingredients in a bowl. The mixture is lifted high and the lumps of fat rubbed between the fingertips as the mixture is allowed to fall back into the bowl.

1 Sift the flour into a bowl, adding the raising agents, salt and any sugar or spices and mix them evenly.

2 Stir in any other dry ingredients; combine the oats or other cereal, or coconut. Add the butter or margarine, cut into pieces.

3 Sprinkle the liquid ingredients (water, cream, milk, buttermilk or beaten egg) over the mixture.

4 Mix with your fingers or stir with a fork until the dry ingredients are thoroughly moistened and will come together in a ball of fairly soft dough in the centre of the bowl.

5 Press the dough into a ball. If it is too dry to form a dough, add some extra water.

6 Turn the dough on to a lightly floured surface. Knead very lightly, folding and pressing, to mix evenly – about 30 seconds. Wrap the ball of dough in clear film or greaseproof paper and chill it for at least 30 minutes.

Making cookies by the creaming method

To make cookies by the creaming method, the fat and sugar are 'creamed' – or beaten – together before the eggs and dry ingredients are added. The fat (usually butter or margarine) should be soft enough to be beaten so, if necessary, remove it from the refrigerator and leave for at least 30 minutes. For best results, the eggs should be at room temperature.

1 Sift the flour with the salt, raising agent(s) and any other dry ingredients, such as spices or cocoa powder, into a bowl. Set aside.

2 Put the fat in a large, deep bowl and beat with an electric mixer at medium speed, or a wooden spoon, until the texture is soft and pliable.

3 Add the sugar to the creamed fat gradually. With the mixer at medium-high speed, or using the wooden spoon, beat it into the fat until the mixture is pale and very fluffy. The sugar should be completely incorporated.

5 Add the dry ingredients to the mixture. Beat at low speed just until smoothly combined, or fold in with a large metal spoon.

6 If the recipe calls for any liquid, add it in small portions alternately with portions of the dry ingredients.

7 If the recipe specifies, whisk egg whites separately until frothy, add sugar and continue whisking until stiff peaks form. Fold into the mixture.

Making cookies by the all-in-one method

Some cookies are made by an easy all-in-one method where all the ingredients are combined in a bowl and beaten thoroughly. The mixture can also be made in a food processor, but take care not to over-process. A refinement on the all-in-one method is to separate the eggs and make the mixture with the yolks. The whites are whisked separately and then folded in. Soft margarine has to be used.

1 Sift the flour and any other dry ingredients such as salt, raising agents and spices, into a bowl.

2 Add the liquid ingredients, such as eggs, melted or soft fat, milk or fruit juices, and beat until smooth, with an electric mixer for speed. Pour into the prepared tins and bake as specified in the recipe.

4 Add the eggs or egg yolks, one at a time, beating well after each addition. Scrape the bowl often so all the ingredients are evenly combined. If the mixture curdles, add 15ml/1 tbsp of the measured flour.

8 Pour the mixture into a prepared cake tin and bake as specified.

Rolling and cutting cookies

A cookie dough that is to be rolled and cut must have the right consistency; if it is too dry it will crumble, crack and be difficult to roll neatly, whereas if it is too wet it will stick when rolled out and will spread during baking.

1 After mixing, knead the cookie dough lightly so it holds together, then wrap it in clear film or greaseproof paper and chill it for at least 1 hour. To speed the chilling, put the dough in the freezer for 30 minutes. Tap over the dough with a rolling pin to flatten it, then gently roll out the dough with short, light strokes in one direction to the required thickness.

2 Doughs that are stiff enough to roll may be cut with a knife into squares, rectangles, triangles or fingers, or they can be stamped into rounds or fancy shapes using cutters. To prevent sticking, sprinkle the work surface generously with flour or sugar, according to the recipe, before rolling out the dough, and use a floured or sugared rolling pin.

3 Position the floured cutter near the outside edge of the dough and cut out the shape. Continue cutting out shapes, each time placing the cutter close to the cut out holes, to minimize trimmings. Carefully transfer to the prepared baking sheet. Glaze with beaten egg and sprinkle with nuts, seeds or cheese, if used.

Shaping drop cookies

1 Drop cookies are made from a number of different mixtures, but they invite the use of coarse-textured oats, nuts and dried fruits that cannot be piped. Drop cookies are very easy to shape; spoonfuls of mixture are simply dropped on to the prepared baking sheet.

2 Leave plenty of space between the cookies because they spread during cooking. If a mixture is quite stiff it will have to be spread with the back of a teaspoon or fork, but this is not usually necessary. Drop teaspoons of the mixture on to the prepared baking sheet, spacing them well apart.

Shaping tuiles & cigarettes

Delicate drop cookies, such as Tuiles d'amandes and Brandy Snaps, can be a challenge to the cook. The mixture is particularly thin and a tablespoon or more of flour or liquid can make the difference between success and failure.

1 Roll spoonfuls of the dough into balls and place 2.5–5cm/1–2in apart on the prepared baking sheets. Press down with a spoon to flatten.

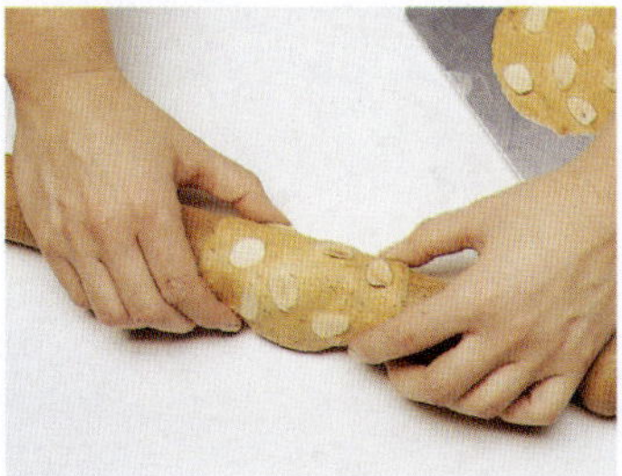

2 Bake until golden brown, 8–10 minutes. Curve tuiles over a rolling pin and roll cigarettes around a wooden spoon handle.

Moulding cookies

Doughs that are too rich to roll out can be shaped by hand. Some recipes call for moistening your hands with water before handling the dough, others recommend lightly flouring your hands, or using cocoa powder or sugar.

1 Take walnut-size pieces of dough and roll into smooth balls between the palms of your hands. Set them spaced well apart on the prepared baking sheet.

2 Flatten the balls with the back of the tines of a wetted fork to give an attractive lined effect. Alternatively, the base of a greased glass dipped in caster or icing sugar can be used.

Making refrigerator cookies

These are so-called because the dough must be thoroughly chilled before it can be cut into slices for baking, or for serving, and also because the dough can be conveniently kept in the refrigerator for up to a week before it is baked. The dough can also be frozen and used straight from the freezer, using a good sharp knife.

Refrigerator cookies are simple to make because the chilled logs are firm and easy to slice. They are also time-saving because you can make the roll ahead and slice off just as many cookies as you need at any time. Use a thin, sharp knife and wet the knife occasionally to help to give a smooth, clean cut.

The thickness of the slices determines the character of baked cookies: very thin slices will bake into thin, crisp cookies; thick slices result in thicker, more chewy cookies. Place 2.5cm/1in apart on the baking sheets, which are usually ungreased.

1 Beat together the butter and sugar until light and fluffy. Add the flour in three batches, folding in well between each addition. Add any other ingredients and stir in gently.

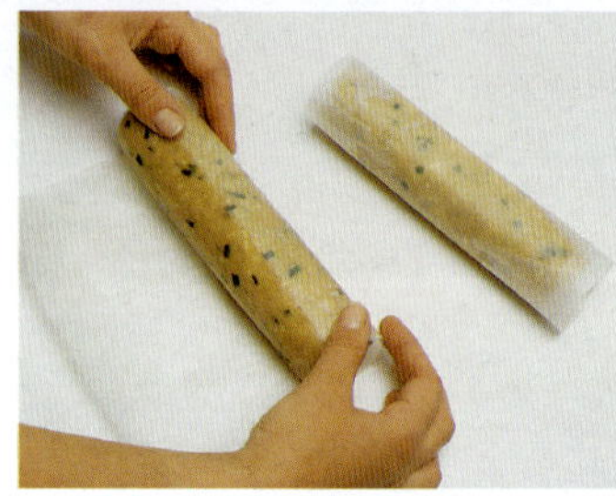

2 Divide the dough in half and shape each half into a log about 5cm/2in in diameter. Wrap in greaseproof paper and chill overnight. Preheat the oven to 190°C/375°F/Gas 5. Lightly grease two baking sheets.

3 Cut the dough logs across into slices about 3mm/⅛in thick. Place on the prepared baking sheets. Bake for about 10 minutes, until just golden around the edges. Transfer to a wire rack to cool.

Piping cookies

The mixture for piped cookies needs to be soft enough to pipe, but it should not be too loose or it will spread and lose its shape during baking. You will need a piping bag of an appropriate size and a large nozzle, either plain or star-shaped, depending on the effect you want to produce (obviously, a star nozzle will give a more decorative appearance). Drop the piping nozzle into the piping bag and twist, tucking the bag into the nozzle. This will prevent any filling from leaking out at the bottom.

1 Fold the top of the bag over your hand to form a collar, or stand the bag in a tall glass. Add the mixture, scraping the spoon or spatula against your hand or the side of the glass. When the bag is one-half to two-thirds full, twist the top until there is no air left.

2 Hold the twisted end of the bag firmly in one hand. Use the other hand to lightly guide the nozzle. Exert a very firm, steady pressure and start to pipe. The trick is to keep the pressure steady until the design is finished. A sudden squeeze will produce a large blob rather than an even flow.

3 As soon as the shape is complete, stop applying pressure, push down slightly and quickly lift up the nozzle.

4 The bag is kept upright for piping swirls, stars or rosettes, but to make straight lines it is held at an angle.

Making a greaseproof-paper icing bag

Greaseproof-paper icing bags are particularly ideal for piping small quantities of icing or when two or more colours of icing are being used at once. They are also easy to use for any type of icing. The bag can be used without a piping nozzle for making simple, plain lines, or it can be fitted with any size of nozzle. It is a good idea to make several of these bags at a time.

1 Cut a piece of good quality greaseproof paper to a 25cm/10in square. Fold in half to form a triangle.

2 Fold the short side of the triangle over to the right-angled corner to form a cone.

3 Holding the cone together with one hand, wrap the long point of the triangle around the paper cone.

4 Tuck the point of paper inside the cone to secure it. For extra security, clear sticky tape can be used to hold the paper together. Add the icing, then cut a small, straight piece off the end of the bag.

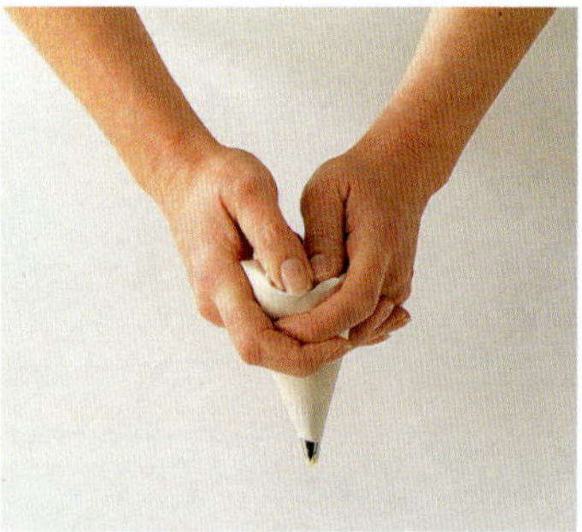

5 For using with a nozzle, cut off the pointed end of the bag and position the nozzle so that it fits snugly into the point before adding the icing.

Tip To use the bag for piping, do not overfill it; instead, open it carefully and refill it when necessary, taking care not to split it or let it unfold. The filled bag can be kept in a plastic bag for a few hours.

Decorating cookies with icing

It is very easy to turn plain cookies into special-looking treats, whether for a children's birthday party or to give as a present to an adult. All that is needed is some icing – you don't even have to do any piping. However, it is a very simple matter to add a little piped icing. There's no need to be adept at icing – the surfaces you will be covering are small so it won't matter if the lines are squiggly.

A very easy way to decorate the tops of cookies is to spread the icing over the top, using a palette knife.

Another very straightforward way to ice or coat cookies is to just dip them in the coating.

Icing glaze This is like glacé icing but is thinned with egg white so that it sets, making a thin, tangy biscuit glaze.

15ml/1 tbsp lightly beaten egg white
15ml/1 tbsp lemon juice
75–115g/3–4oz/$^{3}/_{4}$–1 cup icing sugar
Mix the egg white and lemon juice in a bowl. Gradually beat in the icing sugar, until the mixture is smooth and has the consistency of thin cream. The icing should coat the back of a spoon.

A simple yet effective way to decorate cookies is to pipe lines of a contrasting colour backwards and forwards across the top of the baked cookies. With just a few simple, short lines you can add the finishing touches to some spectacular cookies.

A portion of the raw cookie mixture can be coloured then piped over the shaped, but still unbaked cookies, so the design is cooked in the cookies.

Stencilling

Stencilling is a fun way to liven up cookies. There are no hard and fast rules – experiment with different templates. Cut a small design or initial out of card and place it over a cookie. Dust the cookie with icing sugar or cocoa before carefully removing the card.

Melting chocolate

Melt chocolate slowly, as overheating will spoil both the flavour and texture. Dark chocolate should not be heated above 49°C/120°F; milk and white chocolate should not go above 43°C/110°F. Do not allow water or steam to come into contact with melting chocolate as this may cause it to stiffen. Leave chocolate uncovered, after melting, as condensation could also cause it to stiffen.

Using a double boiler

1 Fill the base of a double boiler or saucepan about a quarter full. Fit the top pan or place a heatproof bowl over the saucepan. The water should not touch the top container. Bring the water to just below boiling point, then turn down the heat to the lowest possible setting.

2 Chop the chocolate or break it into squares and place in the top pan or bowl. Leave to melt completely. Stir until smooth. Keep the water at a very low simmer all the time.

▲ **Using the microwave** Chop the chocolate or break it into squares and place it in a bowl suitable for use in the microwave. Heat until just softened – chocolate burns easily in the microwave, so check often, remembering that chocolate retains its shape when melted in this way.

Approximate times for melting plain or milk chocolate in a 650–700 watt microwave oven are: 115g/4oz, 2 minutes on High (100% power), 200–225g/7–8oz 3 minutes on High (100% power), 115g/4oz white chocolate, 2 minutes on Medium (50% power).

◀ **Using direct heat** This is only suitable for recipes where the chocolate is melted in plenty of other liquid, such as milk or cream. Chop the chocolate or break it into a saucepan. Add the liquid, then heat gently, stirring occasionally, until the chocolate has melted and the mixture is smooth.

Storing cookies

Cookies should always be cooled completely before storing. When stored, crisp cookies tend to go soft, and soft ones can harden and dry out. The key to storing cookies is to choose an airtight container. This could be a jar or tin with a tight-fitting lid, or a rigid plastic box with a close-fitting lid. If you are not quite sure about the fit of a lid, put the cookies in a sealed plastic bag first. Alternatively, cover the top of the tin, jar or container with clear film before putting on the lid.

▲ **Glass jars** Glass jars with airtight stoppers or corks, or screw-topped lids, allow the cookies to be seen. Found mostly in kitchen departments or shops, some jars come in wonderful shapes and colours.

▶ **Tins** Tins make excellent airtight containers for cookies and come in all shapes and sizes. Look for the more unconventional shapes and designs in large stores, kitchen shops and stationers.

Gift-wrapping cookies

Cookies make wonderful gifts, and you can easily make the wrapping as special as the contents for an irresistible present.

▶ **Gift-wrapping materials** The emphasis on attractive gift-wrap has increased considerably in recent years. It is relatively simple to make small gifts at home and package them beautifully. Personalized gifts are as much a joy to give as to receive.

There are many shops that specialize in gift-wrapping materials. Papers, ribbons, different types of boxes, containers, labels and cards are all available. When making your own gifts, look out for unusual accessories with which to enhance the packaging of the fruits of your labours. Keep an eye open for innovative containers in second-hand, bric-a-brac and antique shops and markets.

▲ **Boxes** These make wonderful containers for cookies. You will find many different designs, colours and sizes in stationers, paper specialists or large stores. If your gift will be given, and eaten, quickly, a pretty box lined with tissue paper may be the answer.

▲ **Bags** Paper and fabric bags can be used for cookies that are given and eaten quickly. They come in a variety of sizes and often have a matching gift label attached. A utilitarian brown paper bag undergoes a complete transformation when it is spatter-sprayed with gold and silver paint. Here it is decorated with a trio of candies wired to the ribbon and with gilded hydrangea heads stuck onto one side.

▲ **Cellophane** For a simple yet stylish presentation, wrap neat piles of cookies in cellophane and tie with string or a pretty ribbon.

Many different shapes and types of container make the gift seem that little bit extra special. For a very special gift, choose a fine porcelain dish, cover with cellophane or clear wrap, and tie with a co-ordinating ribbon.

▲ Many different shapes and types of container make the gift seem that little bit extra special.

▶ **Gift cards and tags** These are often available to co-ordinate with your chosen paper, box or container. You can easily make your own tags by sticking your chosen paper on to a plain piece of card before making a hole in the corner and adding a ribbon. The choice of ribbons is overwhelming; even the simplest ribbons can transform a gift more than any other packaging.

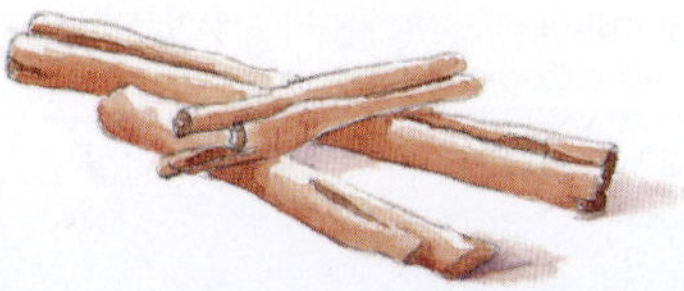

Traditional Cookies

Snickerdoodles, Tollhouse Cookies, Melting Moments, Ginger Cookies, Scottish Shortbread – these are not just cookies but an integral part of a country's national cuisine, even its national heritage. Such cookies are foods we have known, eaten and loved all our lives, so making them can easily result in a trip along memory lane.

Traditional cookies have been made by generations of family and country cooks, usually using local produce, as in Brittany Butter Cookies which come from the rich dairy-land of western France, and Oatmeal Wedges from Scotland. The ingredients are inexpensive, available, everyday items and the methods straightforward.

Cookies will usually keep well; if they lose their freshness or crispness, they can be refreshed in a low oven, about 160°C/325°F/Gas 3 for about three minutes.

It is a good idea to make a large batch of cookie dough and keep some in the freezer, either as a ball of dough, or ready-shaped, depending on the amount of room available, so you can quickly cook some cookies when you need them. Cookies can also be frozen after baking, but after defrosting will need to be refreshed in a low oven for about three minutes before serving.

Granola Cookies

Makes 18

INGREDIENTS

115g/4oz/½ cup butter or margarine
75g/3oz/½ cup light brown sugar
75g/3oz/⅓ cup crunchy peanut butter
1 egg
50g/2oz/½ cup plain flour
2.5ml/½ tsp baking powder
2.5ml/½ tsp ground cinnamon
pinch of salt
225g/8oz/2 cups muesli
50g/2oz/⅓ cup raisins
50g/2oz/½ cup walnuts, chopped

1 Preheat the oven to 180°C/350°F/Gas 4. Grease a baking sheet. Put the butter or margarine in a bowl.

2 With an electric mixer, cream the butter or margarine and sugar until light and fluffy. Beat in the peanut butter, then beat in the egg.

3 Sift the flour, baking powder, cinnamon and salt over the peanut butter mixture and stir to blend. Stir in the muesli, raisins, and walnuts. Taste the mixture to see if it needs more sugar, as mueslis vary in sweetness.

4 Drop rounded tablespoonfuls of the batter on to the prepared baking sheet about 2.5cm/1in apart. Press gently with the back of a spoon to spread each mound into a circle.

5 Bake for about 15 minutes until lightly coloured. With a metal spatula, transfer to a wire rack and leave to cool.

Crunchy Oatmeal Cookies

Makes 14

INGREDIENTS

175g/6oz/¾ cup butter or margarine
125g/4½oz/¾ cup caster sugar
1 egg yolk
175g/6oz/1½ cups plain flour
5ml/1 tsp bicarbonate of soda
pinch of salt
40g/1½oz/½ cup rolled oats
40g/1½oz/½ cup crunchy nugget cereal

Variation For Nutty Oatmeal Cookies, substitute an equal quantity of chopped walnuts or pecans for the cereal, and prepare as described.

1 With an electric mixer, cream the butter or margarine and sugar together until light and fluffy. Mix in the egg yolk.

2 Sift over the flour, bicarbonate of soda and salt, then stir into the butter mixture. Add the oats and cereal and stir to blend. Chill for at least 20 minutes.

3 Preheat the oven to 190°C/375°F/Gas 5. Grease a baking sheet. Flour the bottom of a glass.

4 Roll the dough into balls. Place them on the prepared baking sheet and flatten with the bottom of the glass.

5 Bake for 10–12 minutes until golden. With a metal spatula, transfer to a wire rack to cool completely.

Coconut Oat Cookies

Makes 18

INGREDIENTS

175g/6oz/2 cups quick-cooking oats
75g/3oz/1 cup shredded coconut
225g/8oz/1 cup butter or margarine, at room temperature
115g/4oz/½ cup granulated sugar
40g/1½oz/¼ cup firmly packed dark brown sugar
2 eggs
60ml/4 tbsp milk
7.5ml/1½ tsp vanilla essence
115g/4oz/1 cup plain flour
2.5ml/½ tsp bicarbonate of soda
pinch of salt
5ml/1 tsp ground cinnamon

1 Preheat the oven to 200°C/400°F/Gas 6. Lightly grease two baking sheets. Grease the bottom of a glass and dip in sugar.

2 Spread the oats and coconut on an ungreased baking sheet. Bake for 8–10 minutes until golden brown, stirring occasionally.

3 With an electric mixer, cream the butter or margarine and both sugars until light and fluffy. Beat in the eggs, one at a time, then add the milk and vanilla essence. Sift over the dry ingredients and fold in. Stir in the oats and coconut.

4 Drop spoonfuls of the dough 2.5–5cm/1–2in apart on the baking sheets and flatten with the glass. Bake for 8–10 minutes. Transfer to a wire rack to cool.

Crunchy Jumbles

Makes 36

INGREDIENTS

115g/4oz/½ cup butter or margarine, at room temperature
225g/8oz/1 cup sugar
1 egg
5ml/1 tsp vanilla essence
175g/6oz/1¼ cups plain flour
2.5ml/½ tsp bicarbonate of soda
pinch of salt
115g/4oz/2 cups crisped rice cereal
1 cup chocolate chips

Variation For even crunchier cookies, add ½ cup walnuts, coarsely chopped, with the cereal and chocolate chips.

1 Preheat the oven to 180°C/350°F/Gas 4. Lightly grease two baking sheets.

2 With an electric mixer, cream the butter or margarine and sugar until light and fluffy. Beat in the egg and vanilla. Sift over the flour, bicarbonate of soda, and salt and fold in.

3 Add the cereal and chocolate chips. Stir to mix thoroughly.

4 Drop spoonfuls of the dough 2.5–5cm/1–2in apart on the prepared sheets. Bake for 10–12 minutes until golden. Transfer to a wire rack to cool.

Malted Oaty Crisps

These cookies are very crisp and crunchy – ideal to serve with morning coffee.

Makes 18

INGREDIENTS

175g/6oz/1½ cups rolled oats
75g/3oz/¼ cup light muscovado sugar
1 egg
60ml/4 tbsp sunflower oil
30ml/2 tbsp malt extract

1 Preheat the oven to 190°C/375°F/Gas 5. Lightly grease two baking sheets. Mix the rolled oats and brown sugar in a bowl, breaking up any lumps in the sugar. Add the egg, sunflower oil and malt extract, mix well, then leave to soak for 15 minutes.

2 Using a teaspoon, place small heaps of the mixture well apart on the prepared baking sheets. Press the heaps into 7.5cm/3in rounds with the back of a dampened fork.

3 Bake for 10–15 minutes, until golden brown. Leave to cool for 1 minute, then remove with a palette knife and cool on a wire rack.

Variation To give these crisp biscuits a coarser texture, substitute jumbo oats for some or all of the rolled oats.

Shortbread

Makes 8

INGREDIENTS

175g/6oz/2/3 cup unsalted butter
115g/4oz/1/2 cup caster sugar
150g/5oz/1 1/4 cups plain flour
50g/2oz/1/2 cup rice flour
1.5ml/1/4 tsp baking powder
pinch of salt

1 Preheat the oven to 160°C/325°F/Gas 3. Grease a shallow 20cm/8in cake tin.

2 With an electric mixer, cream the butter and sugar together until light and fluffy. Sift over the flours, baking powder and salt and mix well.

3 Press the dough neatly into the prepared tin, smoothing the surface with the back of a spoon. Prick all over with a fork, then score into eight equal wedges.

4 Bake for 40–45 minutes. Leave in the tin until cool enough to handle, then unmould and recut the wedges while still hot.

Oatmeal Wedges

Makes 8

INGREDIENTS

50g/2oz/4 tbsp butter
25ml/1 1/2 tbsp treacle
50g/2oz/1/3 cup dark brown sugar
175g/6oz/1 1/4 cups rolled oats
pinch of salt

Variation If wished, add 5ml/1 tsp ground ginger to the melted butter.

1 Preheat the oven to 180°C/350°F/Gas 4. Line a 20cm/8in shallow cake tin with greaseproof paper and grease the paper.

2 Place the butter, treacle and sugar in a saucepan over a low heat. Cook, stirring, until melted and combined.

3 Remove from the heat and add the oats and salt. Stir to blend.

4 Spoon into the prepared cake tin and smooth the surface. Bake for 20–25 minutes until golden brown. Leave in the tin until cool enough to handle, then unmould and cut into eight equal wedges while still hot.

Melting Moments

These cookies are very crisp and light – and they melt in your mouth.

Makes 16–20

INGREDIENTS

40g/1½oz/3 tbsp butter or margarine
65g/2½oz/5 tbsp lard
75g/3oz/½ cup caster sugar
½ egg, beaten
few drops of vanilla or almond essence
150g/5oz/1¼ cups self-raising flour
rolled oats for coating
4–5 glacé cherries, quartered

1 Preheat the oven to 180°C/350°F/Gas 4. Grease two baking sheets. Cream together the butter or margarine, lard and sugar, then gradually beat in the egg and vanilla or almond essence.

2 Stir the flour into the beaten mixture, then roll into 16–20 small balls in your hands.

3 Spread the rolled oats on a sheet of greaseproof paper and toss the balls in them to coat evenly.

4 Place the balls, spaced slightly apart, on the prepared baking sheets, place a piece of cherry on top of each and bake for 15–20 minutes, until lightly browned. Allow the cookies to cool for a few minutes before transferring to a wire rack.

Apricot Yogurt Cookies

These soft cookies are very quick to make and are useful for lunch boxes.

Makes 16

INGREDIENTS

175g/6oz/1½ cups plain flour
5ml/1 tsp baking powder
5ml/1 tsp ground cinnamon
75g/3oz/1 cup rolled oats
75g/3oz/½ cup light muscovado sugar
115g/4oz/¾ cup chopped ready-to-eat dried apricots
15ml/1 tbsp flaked hazelnuts or almonds
150g/5oz/⅔ cup natural yogurt
45ml/3 tbsp sunflower oil
demerara sugar, for sprinkling

1 Preheat the oven to 190°C/375°F/Gas 5. Lightly oil a large baking sheet.

2 Sift together the flour, baking powder and cinnamon. Stir in the oats, sugar, apricots and nuts.

Cook's Tip These cookies do not keep well, so it is best to eat them within two days, or to freeze them. Pack into polythene bags and freeze for up to four months.

3 Beat together the yogurt and oil, then stir evenly into the flour mixture to make a firm dough. If necessary, add a little more yogurt. Use your hands to roll the mixture into about 16 small balls.

4 Place the balls on the prepared baking sheet and flatten with a fork. Sprinkle with demerara sugar. Bake for 15–20 minutes, until firm and golden brown. Transfer to a wire rack and leave to cool.

Applesauce Cookies

These fruit-flavoured cookies are a favourite with children.

Makes 36

INGREDIENTS

450g/1lb cooking apples, peeled, cored and chopped
45ml/3 tbsp water
115g/4oz/½ cup caster sugar
115g/4oz/½ cup butter or margarine
115g/4oz/1 cup plain flour
2.5ml/½ tsp baking powder
1.5ml/¼ tsp bicarbonate of soda
pinch of salt
2.5ml/½ tsp ground cinnamon
50g/2oz/½ cup chopped walnuts

1 Cook the apple with the water in a covered saucepan over a low heat until the apple is tender. Cool slightly then purée in a blender or mash with a fork Measure out 175ml/6fl oz/¾ cup.

2 Preheat the oven to 190°C/375°F/ Gas 5. Grease a baking sheet. In a medium-size bowl, cream together the sugar and butter or margarine until well mixed. Beat in the apple sauce.

Cook's Tip If the apple sauce is too runny, put it in a strainer over a bowl and let it drain for 10 minutes before measuring it out.

3 Sift the flour, baking powder, bicarbonate of soda, salt and cinnamon into the mixture, and stir to blend. Fold in the chopped walnuts.

4 Drop teaspoonfuls of the dough on to the prepared baking sheet, spacing them about 5cm/2in apart.

5 Bake the cookies for 8–10 minutes until they are golden brown. Transfer to a wire rack and leave to cool.

Chocolate Chip Hazelnut Cookies

Chocolate chip cookies, with a delicious nutty flavour.

Makes 36

INGREDIENTS

115g/4oz/1 cup plain flour
5ml/1 tsp baking powder
pinch of salt
75g/3oz/⅓ cup butter or margarine
115g/4oz/1½ cups caster sugar
50g/2oz/⅓ cup light brown sugar
1 egg
5ml/1 tsp vanilla essence
125g/4½oz/⅔ cup chocolate chips
50g/2oz/½ cup hazelnuts, chopped

1 Preheat the oven to 180°C/350°F/Gas 4. Grease 2–3 baking sheets. Sift the flour, baking powder and salt into a small bowl. Set aside.

2 With an electric mixer, cream together the butter or margarine and the sugars. Beat in the egg and vanilla essence. Add the flour mixture and beat well with the mixer on low speed.

3 Stir in the chocolate chips and half of the hazelnuts, using a wooden spoon.

4 Drop teaspoonfuls of the mixture on to the prepared baking sheets, to form 2cm/¾in mounds. Space the cookies 2.5–5cm/1–2in apart.

5 Flatten each cookie lightly with a wet fork. Sprinkle the remaining hazelnuts on top of the cookies and press lightly into the surface.

6 Bake for 10–12 minutes until golden. Transfer the biscuits to a wire rack and leave to cool.

Chocolate Chip Oat Biscuits

Makes 60

INGREDIENTS

115g/4oz/1 cup plain flour
2.5ml/½ tsp bicarbonate of soda
1.5ml/¼ tsp baking powder
pinch of salt
115g/4oz/½ cup butter or margarine
115g/4oz/½ cup caster sugar
90g/3½oz/generous ½ cup light brown sugar
1 egg
½ tsp vanilla essence
75g/3oz/¾ cup rolled oats
175g/6oz/1 cup plain chocolate chips

1 Preheat the oven to 180°C/350°F/Gas 4. Grease 3–4 baking sheets.

2 Sift the flour, bicarbonate of soda, baking powder and salt into a mixing bowl. Set aside.

3 With an electric mixer, cream together the butter or margarine and the sugars. Add the egg and vanilla essence and beat until light and fluffy.

4 Add the flour mixture and beat on a low speed until thoroughly blended. Stir in the rolled oats and chocolate chips. The dough should be crumbly. Drop heaped teaspoonfuls on to the prepared baking sheets, spacing the dough about 2.5cm/1in apart.

5 Bake for about 15 minutes until just firm around the edge but still soft to the touch in the centre. With a slotted spatula, transfer the biscuits to a wire rack and leave to cool.

Mexican Almond Cookies

Light and crisp, these biscuits are perfect with a cup of strong coffee.

Makes 24

INGREDIENTS

115g/4oz/1 cup plain flour
175g/6oz/1⅓ cups icing sugar
pinch of salt
50g/2oz/½ cup almonds, finely chopped
2.5ml/½ tsp vanilla essence
115g/4oz/½ cup unsalted butter
icing sugar for dusting

Variation Try using other nuts such as walnuts, peanuts or pecans.

1 Preheat the oven to 180°C/350°F/Gas 4. Sift the flour, icing sugar and salt into a bowl. Add the almonds and mix well. Stir in the vanilla essence.

2 Using your fingertips, work the butter into the mixture to make a dough. Form it into a ball.

3 Roll out the dough on a lightly floured surface until it is 3mm/⅛in thick. Using a round cutter, stamp out into about 24 biscuits, re-rolling the trimmings as necessary.

4 Transfer the biscuits to non-stick baking sheets and bake for 30 minutes, until browned. Transfer to wire racks to cool, then dust thickly with icing sugar.

Peanut Butter Cookies

For extra crunch add 50g/2oz/½ cup chopped peanuts with the peanut butter.

Makes 24

INGREDIENTS

115g/4oz/1 cup plain flour
2.5ml/½ tsp bicarbonate of soda
pinch of salt
115g/4oz/½ cup butter
125g/4½oz/¾ cup firmly packed light brown sugar
1 egg
5ml/1 tsp vanilla essence
225g/8oz/1 cup crunchy peanut butter

1 Sift together the flour, bicarbonate of soda and salt and set aside.

2 With an electric mixer, cream together the butter and sugar until light and fluffy.

3 In another bowl, mix the egg and vanilla essence, then gradually beat into the butter mixture.

4 Stir in the peanut butter and blend thoroughly. Stir in the dry ingredients. Chill for at least 30 minutes, until firm.

5 Preheat the oven to 180°C/350°F/ Gas 4. Grease two baking sheets.

6 Spoon out rounded teaspoonfuls of the dough and roll into balls.

7 Place the balls on the prepared baking sheets and press flat with a fork into circles about 6cm/2½in in diameter, making a criss-cross pattern. Bake for 12–15 minutes, until lightly coloured. Transfer to a wire rack to cool.

Tollhouse Cookies

Makes 24

INGREDIENTS

115g/4oz/½ cup butter or margarine
50g/2oz/¼ cup granulated sugar
75g/3oz/½ cup dark brown sugar
1 egg
2.5ml/½ tsp vanilla essence
125g/4½oz/1⅛ cups flour
2.5ml/½ tsp bicarbonate of soda
pinch of salt
175g/6oz/1 cup chocolate chips
50g/2oz/½ cup walnuts, chopped

1 Preheat the oven to 180°C/350°F/ Gas 4. Grease two baking sheets.

2 With an electric mixer, cream together the butter or margarine and the two sugars until the mixture is light and fluffy.

3 In another bowl, mix the egg and vanilla essence, then gradually beat into the butter mixture. Sift over the flour, bicarbonate of soda and salt. Stir to blend.

4 Add the chocolate chips and walnuts, and mix to combine thoroughly.

5 Place heaped teaspoonfuls of the dough 5cm/2in apart on the prepared baking sheets. Bake for 10–15 minutes until lightly coloured. With a metal spatula, transfer to a wire rack to cool.

Snickerdoodles

Makes 30

INGREDIENTS

115g/4oz/½ cup butter
115g/4oz/1½ cups caster sugar
5ml/1 tsp vanilla essence
2 eggs
50ml/2fl oz/¼ cup milk
400g/14oz/3½ cups plain flour
1 tsp bicarbonate of soda
50g/2oz/½ cup walnuts or pecans, finely chopped
For the coating
75ml/5 tbsp sugar
30ml/2 tbsp ground cinnamon

1 With an electric mixer, beat the butter until light and creamy. Add the sugar and vanilla essence and continue until fluffy. Beat in the eggs, then the milk.

2 Sift the flour and bicarbonate of soda over the butter mixture and stir to blend. Stir in the nuts. Refrigerate for 15 minutes. Preheat the oven to 190°C/375°F/Gas 5. Grease two baking sheets.

3 To make the coating, mix the sugar and cinnamon. Roll tablespoonfuls of the dough into walnut-size balls. Roll the balls in the sugar mixture. You may need to work in batches.

4 Place the balls 5cm/2in apart on the prepared baking sheets and flatten slightly. Bake for about 10 minutes until golden. Transfer to a wire rack to cool.

Chewy Chocolate Cookies

Makes 18

INGREDIENTS

4 egg whites
300g/11oz/2½ cups icing sugar
115g/4oz/1 cup cocoa powder
30ml/2 tbsp plain flour
5ml/1 tsp instant coffee powder
15ml/1 tbsp water
115g/4oz/1 cup walnuts, finely chopped

1 Preheat the oven to 180°C/350°F/Gas 4. Line two baking sheets with greaseproof paper and then grease the paper well.

2 With an electric mixer, beat the egg whites until frothy.

3 Sift the sugar, cocoa, flour and coffee into the whites. Add the water and continue beating on low speed to blend, then on high for a few minutes until the mixture thickens. With a rubber spatula, fold in the walnuts.

4 Place generous spoonfuls of the mixture 2.5cm/1in apart on the prepared baking sheets. Bake for 12–15 minutes until firm and cracked on top but soft on the inside. With a metal spatula, transfer to a wire rack to cool.

Variation Add 75g/3oz/½ cup chocolate chips to the dough with the chopped walnuts.

Buttermilk Cookies

Makes 15

INGREDIENTS

175g/6oz/$1\frac{1}{2}$ cups plain flour
pinch of salt
5ml/1 tsp baking powder
2.5ml/$\frac{1}{2}$ tsp bicarbonate of soda
50g/2oz/4 tbsp cold butter or margarine
175ml/6fl oz/$\frac{3}{4}$ cup buttermilk

1 Preheat the oven to 220°C/425°F/ Gas 7. Grease a baking sheet.

2 Sift the dry ingredients into a bowl. Rub in the butter or margarine until the mixture resembles coarse crumbs.

3 Gradually pour in the buttermilk, stirring with a fork until the mixture forms a soft dough.

4 Roll out to about 1cm/$\frac{1}{2}$in thick. Stamp out 15 5cm/2in circles with a biscuit cutter.

5 Place on the prepared baking sheet and bake for 12–15 minutes until golden. Serve warm or at room temperature.

Baking Powder Cookies

These make a simple accompaniment to meals, or a snack with fruit preserves.

Makes 8

INGREDIENTS

165g/$5\frac{1}{2}$oz/$1\frac{1}{3}$ cups plain flour
30ml/2 tbsp sugar
15ml/1 tbsp baking powder
pinch of salt
40g/$1\frac{1}{2}$oz/5 tbsp cold butter, chopped
120ml/4fl oz/$\frac{1}{2}$ cup milk

Variation For Berry Shortcake, split the cookies in half while still warm. Butter one half, top with lightly sugared fresh berries, such as strawberries, raspberries or blueberries, and sandwich with the other half. Serve with dollops of whipped cream.

1 Preheat the oven to 220°C/425°F/ Gas 7. Grease a baking sheet. Sift the flour, sugar, baking powder and salt into a bowl.

2 Rub in the butter until the mixture resembles coarse crumbs. Pour in the milk and stir with a fork to form a soft dough.

3 Roll out the dough to about 5mm/$\frac{1}{4}$in thick. Stamp out circles with a 6cm/$2\frac{1}{2}$in biscuit cutter.

4 Place on the prepared baking sheet and bake for about 12 minutes, until golden. Serve these soft biscuits hot or warm, spread with butter for meals. To accompany tea or coffee, serve with butter and jam or honey.

Traditional Sugar Cookies

Makes 36

INGREDIENTS

350g/12oz/3 cups plain flour
5ml/1 tsp bicarbonate of soda
10ml/2 tsp baking powder
2.5ml/½ tsp grated nutmeg
115g/4oz/½ cup butter or margarine
225g/8oz/1 cup caster sugar
2.5ml/½ tsp vanilla essence
1 egg
115g/4oz/½ cup milk
coloured or demerara sugar for sprinkling

1 Sift the flour, bicarbonate of soda, baking powder and nutmeg into a small bowl. Set aside.

2 With an electric mixer, cream together the butter or margarine, caster sugar and vanilla essence until the mixture is light and fluffy. Add the egg and beat to mix well.

3 Add the flour mixture alternately with the milk to make a soft dough. Wrap in clear film and chill for at least 30 minutes.

4 Preheat the oven to 180°C/350°F/Gas 4. Roll out the dough on a lightly floured surface to 3mm/⅛in thick. Cut into rounds or other shapes with floured biscuit cutters.

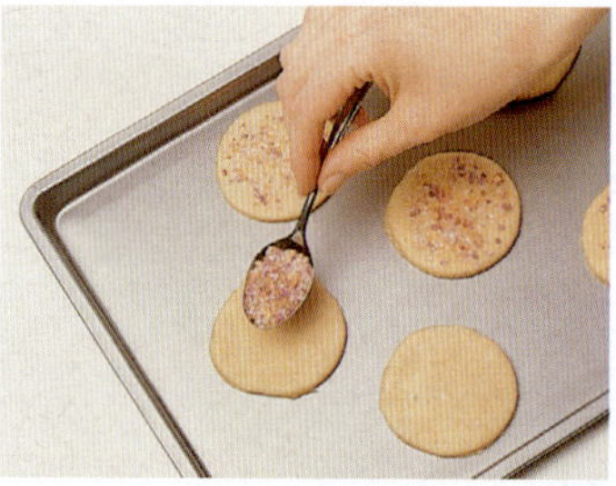

5 Transfer to ungreased baking sheets. Sprinkle with sugar. Bake for 10–12 minutes until golden brown. Transfer the cookies to a wire rack to cool.

Brittany Butter Cookies

These little biscuits are similar to shortbread, but richer. Traditionally, they are made with lightly salted butter.

Makes 18–20

INGREDIENTS

6 egg yolks, lightly beaten
15ml/1 tbsp milk
250g/9 oz/2¼ cups plain flour
175g/6oz/¾ cup caster sugar
200g/7oz/scant 1 cup butter

1 Preheat the oven to 180°C/350°F/ Gas 4. Butter a heavy baking sheet. Mix 15ml/1 tbsp of the egg yolks with the milk to make a glaze.

2 Sift the flour into a bowl. Add the egg yolks, sugar and butter, and work them together until creamy.

3 Gradually bring in a little flour at a time until it forms a slightly sticky dough.

4 Using floured hands, pat out the dough to about 5mm/¼in thick and cut out rounds using a 7.5cm/3in cutter. Transfer the rounds to the prepared baking sheet, brush each with a little egg glaze, then, using the back of a knife, score with lines to create a lattice pattern.

5 Bake for about 12–15 minutes, until golden. Cool in the tin on a wire rack for 15 minutes, then carefully remove the biscuits and leave to cool completely on the rack.

Cook's Tip To make a large Brittany Butter Cake, pat the dough with well-floured hands into a 23cm/9in loose-based cake tin or springform tin. Brush with egg glaze and score the lattice pattern on top. Bake for 45 minutes–1 hour, until firm to the touch and golden brown.

Toffee Cookies

Makes 36

INGREDIENTS

175g/6oz/¾ cup unsalted butter, melted
200g/7oz/1¾ cups instant porridge oats
115g/4oz/packed ½ cup soft light brown sugar
120ml/4fl oz/½ cup corn syrup
30ml/2 tbsp vanilla essence
large pinch of salt
175g/6oz/¾ cup plain chocolate, grated
40g/1½oz/⅓ cup chopped walnuts

1 Preheat the oven to 200°C/400°F/ Gas 6. Grease a 37.5 x 25cm/15 x 10in baking tin.

2 Mix together the butter, oats, sugar, syrup, vanilla essence and salt and press into the prepared tin. Bake for about 15–18 minutes, until the mixture is brown and bubbly.

3 Remove from the oven and immediately sprinkle on the chocolate. Set aside for 10 minutes, then spread the chocolate over the base. Sprinkle on the nuts. Transfer to a wire rack to cool. Cut into squares.

Rosewater Thins

These light, crunchy biscuits are easy to make and bake in minutes.

Makes 60

INGREDIENTS

225g/8oz/1 cup slightly salted butter
225g/8oz/1 cup caster sugar
1 egg
15ml/1 tbsp single cream
300g/11oz/2½ cups plain flour
pinch of salt
5ml/1 tsp baking powder
15ml/1 tbsp rosewater
caster sugar for sprinkling

1 Preheat the oven to 190°C/375°F/ Gas 5. Line two baking sheets with non-stick baking paper.

2 Soften the butter and mix with all the other ingredients until you have a firm dough. Mould the mixture into an even roll and wrap in greaseproof paper. Chill until it is firm enough to slice very thinly. This will take 1–1½ hours.

3 Arrange the cookies on the prepared baking sheets with enough space for them to spread. Sprinkle with a little caster sugar and bake for about 10 minutes until they are just turning brown at the edges.

Scottish Shortbread

Light, crisp shortbread looks very professional when shaped in a mould, although you could also shape it by hand.

Makes 2 large or 8 individual shortbreads

INGREDIENTS

175g/6oz/¾ cup plain flour
50g/2oz/½ cup cornflour
50g/2oz/¼ cup caster sugar, plus extra for sprinkling
115g/4oz/½ cup unsalted butter, chopped

1 Preheat the oven to 160°C/325°F/Gas 3. Lightly flour the mould and line a baking sheet with non-stick baking paper. Sift the flour, cornflour and sugar into a mixing bowl. Rub the butter into the flour mixture until it binds together and you can knead it into a soft dough.

2 Place the dough into the mould and press to fit neatly. Invert the mould on to the baking sheet and tap firmly to release the dough shape. Bake for 35–40 minutes, until pale golden in colour.

3 Sprinkle the top of the shortbread with a little caster sugar and cool on the baking sheet. Wrap in cellophane paper or place in a box tied with ribbon to make a delicious hogmanay gift.

Spanish Churros

Makes 24

INGREDIENTS

250ml/8fl oz/1 cup water
15ml/1 tbsp granulated sugar, plus extra for coating
pinch of salt
175g/6oz/1½ cups plain flour
1 egg
oil for deep frying
½ lime or lemon

Cook's Tip A funnel can be used to shape the churros. Close the end with a finger, add the batter, then release into the oil in small columns.

1 Bring the water, sugar and salt to the boil. Remove from the heat and beat in the flour until smooth.

2 Beat in the egg, using a wooden spoon, until the mixture is smooth and satiny. Set the batter aside.

3 Pour the oil into a deep frying pan to a depth of about 5cm/2in. Add the lime or lemon, then heat the oil to 190°C/375°F, until a cube of day-old bread added to the oil browns in 30–60 seconds.

4 Pour the batter into a piping bag fitted with a fluted nozzle. Pipe 7.5cm/3in strips of batter and then add to the oil, a few at a time. Fry for 3–4 minutes, until golden brown.

5 Using a slotted spoon, remove the churros from the pan and drain on kitchen paper. Roll the hot churros in granulated sugar before serving with a cup of thick hot chocolate.

Golden Pillows

Makes 30

INGREDIENTS

225g/8oz/2 cups plain flour, sifted
15ml/1 tbsp baking powder
pinch of salt
30ml/2 tbsp lard or margarine
175ml/6fl oz/¾ cup water
corn oil for frying
syrup or honey, to serve

Cook's Tip Use your imagination when deciding what to serve with the pillows. Sprinkle them with cinnamon and sugar, or syrup flavoured with rum.

1 Put the flour, baking powder and salt into a large bowl. Lightly rub in the lard or margarine, using your fingertips, until the mixture resembles coarse breadcrumbs.

2 Gradually stir in the water, using a fork, until the mixture clings together to form a soft dough.

3 Shape the dough into a ball, then turn on to a lightly floured surface and knead very gently until smooth. Roll out thinly to a rectangle measuring about 46 x 35cm/18 x 15in. Using a sharp knife, carefully cut about 30 7.5cm/3in squares. For a decorative edge, use a pastry wheel to cut out the squares.

4 Heat the oil to 190°C/375°F, until a cube of day-old bread browns in 30–60 seconds.

5 Fry the squares, a few at a time, in the oil. As they brown and puff up, turn over to cook the other side. Remove with a slotted spoon and drain on kitchen paper. It is important that the temperature of the oil remains constant during the cooking process. Serve warm, with syrup or honey.

Chunky Chocolate Drops

Do not allow these cookies to cool completely on the baking sheet or they will become too crisp and will break when you try to lift them.

Makes 18

INGREDIENTS

175g/6oz plain chocolate, chopped
115g/4oz/½ cup unsalted butter, chopped
2 eggs
90g/3½oz/½ cup granulated sugar
50g/2oz/⅓ cup light brown sugar
40g/1½oz/⅓ cup plain flour
25g/1oz/¼ cup cocoa powder
5ml/1 tsp baking powder
10ml/2 tsp vanilla essence
pinch of salt
115g/4oz/1 cup pecans, toasted and coarsely chopped
175g/6oz/1 cup plain chocolate chips
115g/4oz fine quality white chocolate, chopped into 5mm/¼in pieces
115g/4oz fine quality milk chocolate, chopped into 5mm/¼in pieces

1 Preheat the oven to 160°C/325°F/Gas 3. Grease two large baking sheets. In a medium saucepan over a low heat, melt the plain chocolate and butter, stirring until smooth. Remove from the heat and set aside to cool slightly.

2 In a large mixing bowl, using an electric mixer, beat the eggs and sugars for 2–3 minutes, until pale and creamy. Gradually pour in the melted chocolate mixture, beating until well blended. Beat in the flour, cocoa powder, baking powder, vanilla essence and salt until just blended. Stir in the nuts, chocolate chips and chocolate pieces.

3 Drop heaped tablespoons of the mixture on to the prepared baking sheets 10cm/4in apart. Flatten each to 7.5cm/3in rounds. Bake for 8–10 minutes, until the tops are shiny and cracked and the edges look crisp; do not over-bake or the cookies will become fragile.

4 Remove the baking sheets to a wire rack to cool for 2 minutes, then transfer to the rack to cool completely.

Chocolate Marzipan Cookies

These crisp little cookies satisfy a sweet tooth and have a little almond surprise inside.

Makes 36

INGREDIENTS

200g/7oz/scant 1 cup unsalted butter
200g/7oz/generous 1 cup light muscovado sugar
1 egg
300g/11oz/2½ cups plain flour
60ml/4 tbsp cocoa powder
200g/7oz white almond paste
115g/4oz white chocolate, chopped

1 Preheat the oven to 190°C/375°F/Gas 5. Lightly grease two large baking sheets. Cream the butter with the sugar in a bowl until pale and fluffy. Add the egg and beat well.

2 Sift the flour and cocoa over the mixture. Stir in, first with a wooden spoon, then with clean hands, pressing the mixture together to make a fairly soft dough.

3 Roll out about half the dough on a lightly floured surface to a thickness of about 5mm/¼in. Using a 5cm/2in biscuit cutter, cut out rounds, re-rolling the dough as required until you have about 36 rounds.

4 Cut the almond paste into about 36 equal pieces. Roll into balls, flatten slightly and place one on each round of dough. Roll out the remaining dough, cut out more rounds, then place on top of the almond paste. Press the dough edges to seal. Bake for 10–12 minutes until the cookies have risen well. Cool completely. Melt the white chocolate, spoon into a paper piping bag and pipe on to the biscuits.

Cook's Tip If the dough is too sticky to roll, chill it for about 30 minutes, then try again.

Double Chocolate Cookies

Keep these luscious treats under lock and key unless you're feeling generous.

Makes 18–20

INGREDIENTS

115g/4oz/½ cup unsalted butter
115g/4oz/⅔ cup light muscovado sugar
1 egg
5ml/1 tsp vanilla essence
150g/5oz/1¼ cups self-raising flour
75g/3oz/¾ cup porridge oats
115g/4oz plain chocolate, roughly chopped
115g/4oz white chocolate, roughly chopped

Cook's Tip If you're short of time when making the cookies, substitute chocolate chips for the chopped chocolate. Chopped stem ginger would make a delicious addition as well.

1 Preheat the oven to 190°C/375°F/Gas 5. Lightly grease two baking sheets. Cream the butter with the sugar in a bowl until pale and fluffy. Add the egg and vanilla essence and beat well.

2 Sift the flour over the mixture and fold in lightly with a metal spoon, then add the oats and chopped plain and white chocolate and stir until evenly mixed.

3 Place small spoonfuls of the mixture in 18–20 rocky heaps on the prepared baking sheets, leaving space for spreading.

4 Bake for 15–20 minutes, until beginning to turn pale golden. Cool for 2–3 minutes on the baking sheets, then transfer to wire racks to cool completely.

Chocolate and Nut Refrigerator Cookies

The dough must be chilled thoroughly before it can be sliced and baked.

Makes 50

INGREDIENTS

225g/8oz/2 cups plain flour
pinch of salt
50g/2oz plain chocolate, chopped
225g/8oz/1 cup unsalted butter
225g/8oz/1 cup caster sugar
2 eggs
5ml/1 tsp vanilla essence
115g/4oz/1 cup walnuts, finely chopped

Variation For two-tone cookies, melt only 25g/1oz chocolate. Combine all the ingredients, except the chocolate, as above. Divide the dough in half. Add the chocolate to one half. Roll out the plain dough on to a flat sheet. Roll out the chocolate dough, place on top of the plain dough and roll up. Wrap, slice and bake as described.

1 In a small bowl, sift together the flour and salt. Set aside. Melt the chocolate in the top of a double boiler, or in a heatproof bowl set over a saucepan of hot water. Set aside.

2 With an electric mixer, cream the butter until soft. Add the sugar and continue beating until the mixture is light and fluffy.

3 Mix the eggs with the vanilla essence, then gradually stir into the butter mixture.

4 Stir in the chocolate, then the flour followed by the nuts.

5 Divide the dough into four parts, and roll each into 5cm/2in diameter logs. Wrap tightly in foil and chill or freeze until firm.

6 Preheat the oven to 190°C/375°F/Gas 5. Grease two baking sheets. Cut the dough into 5mm/¼in slices. Place on the prepared sheets and bake for about 10 minutes. Transfer to wire rack to cool.

Chocolate Kisses

These rich little cookies look attractive mixed together on a plate and dusted with icing sugar. Serve them with ice cream or simply with coffee.

Makes 24

INGREDIENTS

75g/3oz plain chocolate, chopped
75g/3oz white chocolate, chopped
115g/4oz/½ cup butter
115g/4oz/½ cup caster sugar
2 eggs
225g/8oz/2 cups plain flour
icing sugar, to decorate

1 Put each chocolate into a small bowl and melt it over a saucepan of hot, but not boiling, water, stirring until smooth. Set aside to cool.

2 Whisk together the butter and caster sugar until pale and fluffy. Beat in the eggs, one at a time.

3 Sift the flour over the butter, sugar and egg mixture and mix in thoroughly.

4 Halve the mixture and divide it between the two bowls of chocolate. Mix each chocolate in well. Knead the doughs until smooth, wrap them in clear film and chill for 1 hour. Preheat the oven to 190°C/375°F/Gas 5. Grease two baking sheets.

5 Shape slightly rounded teaspoonfuls of both doughs roughly into balls. Roll the balls in the palms of your hands to make neater ball shapes. Arrange the balls on the prepared baking sheets and bake for 10–12 minutes. Dust with sifted icing sugar and then transfer to a wire rack to cool.

Chocolate Pretzels

Makes 28

INGREDIENTS

115g/4oz/1 cup plain flour
pinch of salt
45ml/3 tbsp cocoa powder
115g/4oz/½ cup butter
150g/5oz/⅔ cup caster sugar
1 egg
1 egg white, lightly beaten, for glazing
sugar crystals for sprinkling

1 Sift together the flour, salt and cocoa powder. Set aside. Grease two baking sheets.

2 With an electric mixer, cream the butter until light. Add the sugar and continue beating until light and fluffy. Beat in the egg. Add the dry ingredients and stir to blend. Gather the dough into a ball, wrap in greaseproof paper, and chill for 1 hour, or freeze for 30 minutes.

3 Roll the dough into 28 small balls. If the dough is sticky, flour your hands. Chill the balls until needed. Preheat the oven to 190°C/375°F/Gas 5.

4 Roll each ball into a rope about 25cm/10in long. With each rope, form a loop with the two ends facing you. Twist the ends and fold back on to the circle, pressing in to make a pretzel shape. Place on the prepared baking sheets.

5 Brush the pretzels with the egg white. Sprinkle sugar crystals over the tops and bake for 10–12 minutes until firm. Transfer to a wire rack to cool.

Chocolate, Maple and Walnut Swirls

Makes 12

INGREDIENTS

450g/1lb/4 cups strong white flour
2.5ml/½ tsp ground cinnamon
50g/2oz/4 tbsp unsalted butter, chopped
50g/2oz/¼ cup caster sugar
1 sachet easy-blend dried yeast
1 egg yolk
120g/4fl oz/½ cup water
60ml/4 tbsp milk
45ml/3 tbsp maple syrup, to finish
For the filling
40g/1½oz/3 tbsp unsalted butter, melted
50g/2oz/¼ packed cup light muscovado sugar
175g/6oz/1 cup plain chocolate chips
75g/3oz/¾ cup chopped walnuts

1 Grease a deep 23cm/9in springform cake tin. Sift the flour and cinnamon into a bowl, then rub in the butter until the mixture resembles coarse breadcrumbs.

2 Stir in the sugar and yeast. In a jug, beat the egg yolk, with the water and milk, then stir into the dry ingredients to make a soft dough.

3 Knead until smooth, then roll out to about 40 x 30cm/16 x 12in. Brush with melted butter.

4 To make the filling, sprinkle with the muscovado sugar, plain chocolate chips and chopped walnuts.

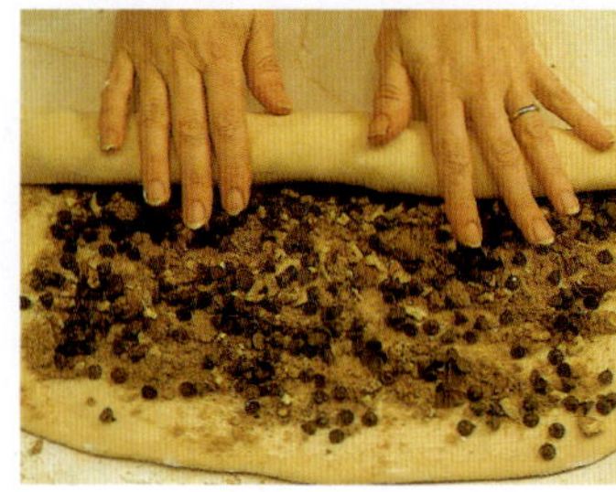

5 Roll up the dough from a long side like a Swiss roll, then cut into 12 thick even-size slices.

6 Pack the slices closely together in the prepared cake tin. Cover and leave in a warm place for 1½ hours, until well risen and springy to the touch. Preheat the oven to 220°C/425°F/Gas 7.

7 Bake for 30–35 minutes, until well risen, golden brown and firm. Remove from the tin and transfer to a wire rack. To finish, spoon the maple syrup over the cake. Pull the pieces apart to serve.

Cook's Tip The amount of liquid added to the dry ingredients may have to be adjusted slightly as some flours absorb more liquid than others.

Old-fashioned Ginger Cookies

Makes 60

INGREDIENTS

300g/11oz/2½ cups plain flour
5ml/1 tsp bicarbonate of soda
7.5ml/1½ tsp ground ginger
1.5ml/¼ tsp ground cinnamon
1.5ml/¼ tsp ground cloves
115g/4oz/½ cup butter or margarine
350g/12oz/1½ cups caster sugar
1 egg, beaten
60ml/4 tbsp black treacle
5ml/1 tsp fresh lemon juice

1 Preheat the oven to 160°C/325°F/Gas 3. Grease 3–4 baking trays.

2 Sift the flour, bicarbonate of soda and spices into a small bowl. Set aside.

3 With an electric mixer, cream together the butter or margarine and two-thirds of the sugar.

4 Stir in the egg, treacle and lemon juice. Add the flour mixture and mix in thoroughly with a wooden spoon to make a soft dough.

5 Shape the dough into 2cm/¾ in balls. Roll the balls in the remaining sugar and place them about 5cm/2in apart on the prepared baking trays.

6 Bake for about 12 minutes until the biscuits are just firm to the touch. With a slotted spatula, transfer the biscuits to a wire rack and leave to cool.

Double Gingerbread Cookies

Packed in little bags or into a gingerbread box, these pretty cookies would make a lovely gift. They are easy to make, but will have everyone wondering how you did it!

Makes 25

INGREDIENTS

For the golden gingerbread mixture
175g/6oz plain flour
1.5ml/1/4 tsp bicarbonate of soda
pinch of salt
5ml/1 tsp ground cinnamon
65g/2 1/2oz unsalted butter, cut in pieces
75g/3oz caster sugar
30ml/2 tbsp maple or golden syrup
1 egg yolk, beaten
For the chocolate gingerbread mixture
175g/6oz/1 1/2 cups plain flour
pinch of salt
10ml/2 tsp ground mixed spice
2.5ml/1/2 tsp bicarbonate of soda
25g/1oz/4 tbsp cocoa powder
75g/3oz/1/3 cup unsalted butter, chopped
75g/3oz/1/3 cup light muscovado sugar
1 egg, beaten

1 To make the golden gingerbread mixture, sift together the flour, bicarbonate of soda, salt and spices. Rub the butter into the flour in a large bowl, until the mixture resembles fine breadcrumbs. Add the sugar, syrup and egg yolk and mix to a firm dough. Knead lightly. Wrap in clear film and chill for 30 minutes before shaping.

2 To make the chocolate gingerbread mixture, sift together the flour, salt, spice, bicarbonate of soda and cocoa powder. Knead the butter into the flour in a large bowl. Add the sugar and egg and mix to a firm dough. Knead lightly. Wrap in clear film and chill for 30 minutes.

3 Roll out half of the chocolate dough on a floured surface to a 28 x 4cm/11 x 1 1/2in rectangle, 1cm/1/2in thick. Repeat with half of the golden gingerbread dough. Using a knife, cut both lengths into seven long, thin strips. Lay the strips together, side by side, alternating the colours.

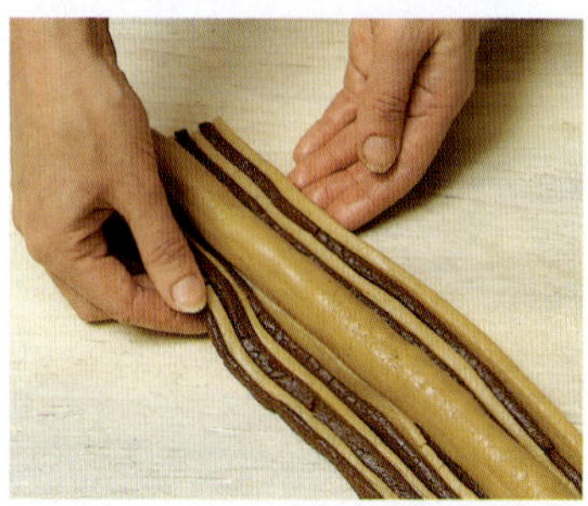

4 Roll out the remaining golden gingerbread dough with your hands to a long sausage, 2cm/3/4in wide and the length of the strips. Lay the sausage of dough down the centre of the striped dough.

5 Carefully bring the striped dough up around the sausage and press it gently in position, to enclose the sausage completely. Roll the remaining chocolate dough to a thin rectangle measuring approximately 28 x 13cm/11 x 5in.

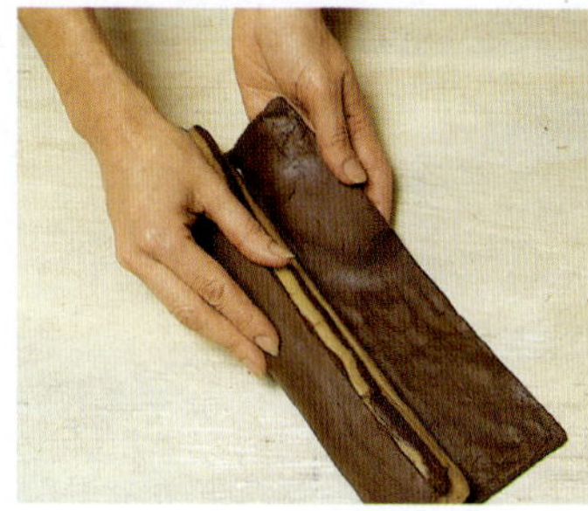

6 Bring the chocolate dough up around the striped dough, to enclose it. Press gently into place. Wrap and chill for 30 minutes.

7 Preheat the oven to 180°C/350°F/Gas 4. Grease a large baking sheet. Cut the gingerbread roll into thin slices and place them, slightly apart, on the prepared baking sheet.

8 Bake for about 12–15 minutes, until just beginning to colour around the edges. Leave on the baking sheet for 3 minutes and transfer to a wire rack to cool completely.

Chocolate Cinnamon Tuiles

Makes 12

INGREDIENTS

1 egg white
50g/2oz/¼ cup caster sugar
30ml/2 tbsp plain flour
40g/1½oz/3 tbsp butter, melted
15ml/1 tbsp cocoa powder
2.5ml/½ tsp ground cinnamon

Cook's Tip Work as quickly as possible when removing the tuiles from the baking sheets – if they firm up too quickly, pop the baking sheet back in the oven for a minute and try again.

1 Preheat the oven to 200°C/400°F/Gas 6. Lightly grease two large baking sheets. Whisk the egg white in a clean, grease-free bowl until it forms soft peaks. Gradually whisk in the sugar to make a smooth, glossy mixture.

2 Sift the flour over the mixture and fold in evenly. Stir in the butter. Transfer about 45ml/3 tbsp of the mixture to a small bowl and set aside.

3 In a separate bowl, mix together the cocoa and cinnamon. Stir into the larger quantity of mixture.

4 Leaving room for spreading, drop spoonfuls of the chocolate-flavoured mixture on to the prepared baking sheets, then spread each gently with a palette knife to make a neat round.

5 Using a small spoon, drizzle the reserved plain mixture over the rounds to give a marbled effect.

6 Bake for 4–6 minutes, until just set. Using a palette knife, lift each biscuit carefully and quickly drape it over a rolling pin, to give a curved shape as it hardens.

7 Leave the tuiles to cool until set, then remove them gently and finish cooling on a wire rack. Serve on the same day.

Spiced-nut Palmiers

Makes 40

INGREDIENTS

75g/3oz/$^{2}/_{3}$ cup chopped almonds, walnuts or hazelnuts
30ml/2 tbsp caster sugar, plus extra for sprinkling
2.5ml/$^{1}/_{2}$ tsp ground cinnamon
225g/8oz rough-puff or puff pastry, defrosted if frozen
1 egg, lightly beaten

1 Lightly butter two large baking sheets, preferably non-stick. In a food processor fitted with a metal blade, process the nuts, sugar and cinnamon until finely ground.

2 Sprinkle the work surface with sugar and roll out the pastry to a 50 x 20cm/20 x 8in rectangle about 3mm/$^{1}/_{8}$in thick. Brush the pastry lightly with beaten egg and sprinkle evenly with half of the nut mixture.

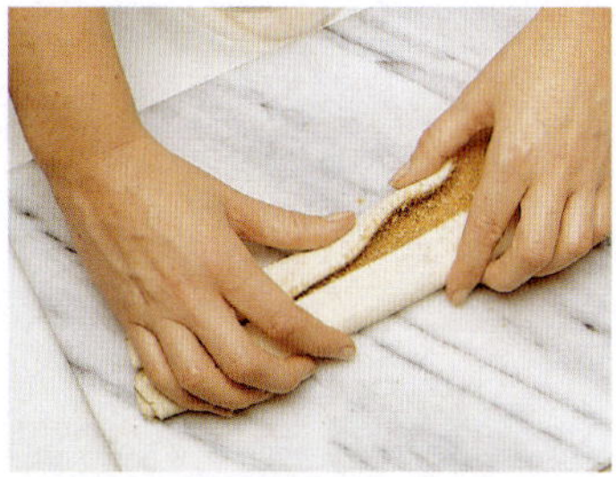

3 Fold in the long edges of the pastry to meet in the centre and flatten with the rolling pin. Brush with egg and sprinkle with most of the nut mixture. Fold in the edges again to meet in the centre, brush with egg and sprinkle with the remaining nut mixture. Fold one side of the pastry over the other.

4 Cut the pastry crossways into 8mm/$^{3}/_{8}$in thick slices and place about 2.5cm/1in apart on the baking sheets.

5 Spread the pastry edges apart to form a wedge shape. Chill the palmiers for at least 15 minutes. Preheat the oven to 220°C/425°F/Gas 7.

6 Bake for about 8–10 minutes, until golden. Carefully turn them over halfway through the cooking time. Keep an eye on them as the sugar can easily scorch. Transfer to a wire rack to cool.

Cinnamon and Treacle Cookies

These cookies are slightly moist, spicy and nutty.

Makes 24

INGREDIENTS

30ml/2 tbsp black treacle
50g/2oz/4 tbsp butter or margarine
115g/4oz/1 cup plain flour
1.5ml/¼ tsp bicarbonate of soda
2.5ml/½ tsp ground ginger
5ml/1 tsp ground cinnamon
40g/1½oz packed cup soft brown sugar
15ml/1 tbsp ground almonds or hazelnuts
1 egg yolk
115g/4oz/1 cup icing sugar, sifted

1 Lightly grease a baking sheet. Heat the treacle and butter or margarine gently until just beginning to melt.

2 Sift the flour into a large bowl with the bicarbonate of soda and spices, then stir in the sugar and almonds or hazelnuts.

3 Beat the treacle mixture and egg yolk briskly into the bowl, drawing the ingredients together to form a firm but soft dough.

4 Roll out the dough on a lightly floured surface to 5mm/¼in thick and stamp out shapes, such as stars, hearts or circles. Re-roll the trimmings and cut more shapes. Place on the prepared baking sheet and chill for 15 minutes.

5 Preheat the oven to 190°C/375°F/Gas 5. Prick the cookies lightly with a fork and bake for 12–15 minutes, until just firm. Transfer to wire racks to become crisp.

6 Mix the icing sugar with a little lukewarm water to make it slightly runny, then drizzle it over the biscuits on the wire racks.

Cinnamon Refrigerator Cookies

Makes 50

INGREDIENTS

225g/8oz/2 cups flour
pinch of salt
10ml/2 tsp ground cinnamon
225g/8oz/1 cup unsalted butter
225g/8oz/1 cup caster sugar
2 eggs
5ml/1 tsp vanilla essence

1 In a bowl, sift together the flour, salt and cinnamon. Set aside.

2 With an electric mixer, cream the butter until soft. Add the sugar and continue beating until the mixture is light and fluffy.

3 Beat together the eggs and vanilla essence, then gradually stir into the butter mixture.

4 Add the dry ingredients to the butter mixture and stir together until evenly combined.

5 Divide the dough into four parts, then roll each into 5cm/2in diameter logs. Wrap tightly in foil and chill or freeze until firm.

6 Preheat the oven to 190°C/375°F/Gas 5. Grease two baking sheets.

7 With a sharp knife, cut the dough into 5mm/¼in slices. Place the rounds on the prepared baking sheets and bake for about 10 minutes until lightly coloured. With a metal spatula, transfer to a wire rack to cool completely.

Spicy Pepper Biscuits

Makes 48

INGREDIENTS

200g/7oz/1¾ cups plain flour
50g/2oz/½ cup cornflour
10ml/2 tsp baking powder
2.5ml/½ tsp ground cardamom
2.5ml/½ tsp ground cinnamon
2.5ml/½ tsp grated nutmeg
2.5ml/½ tsp ground ginger
2.5ml/½ tsp ground allspice
pinch of salt
2.5ml/½ tsp freshly ground black pepper
225g/8oz/1 cup butter or margarine
90g/3½oz/1⅓ cups light brown sugar
2.5ml/½ tsp vanilla essence
5ml/1 tsp finely grated lemon rind
50ml/2fl oz/¼ cup whipping cream
75g/3oz/¾ cup finely ground almonds
30ml/2 tbsp icing sugar

1 Preheat the oven to 180°C/350°F/ Gas 4.

2 Sift the flour, cornflour, baking powder, spices, salt and pepper into a bowl. Set aside.

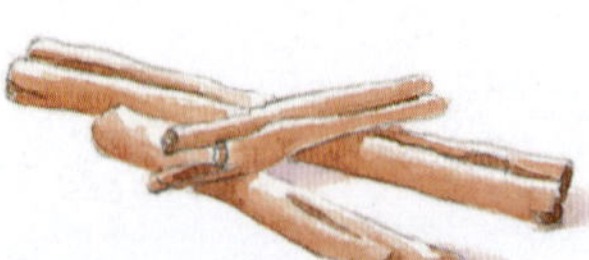

3 With an electric mixer, cream the butter or margarine and brown sugar together until light and fluffy. Beat in the vanilla essence and grated lemon rind.

4 With the mixer on low speed, add the flour mixture alternately with the whipping cream, beginning and ending with flour. Stir in the ground almonds.

5 Shape the dough into 2cm/¾in balls. Place them on ungreased baking sheets, about 2.5cm/1in apart. Bake for 15–20 minutes until golden brown underneath.

6 Leave to cool on the baking sheets for about 1 minute before transferring to a wire rack to cool completely. Before serving, sprinkle lightly with icing sugar.

Lavender Heart Cookies

In folklore, lavender has always been linked with love, as has food, so make some heart-shaped cookies and serve them on Valentine's Day or any other romantic anniversary.

Makes 16–18

INGREDIENTS

115g/4oz/½ cup unsalted butter
50g/2oz/¼ cup caster sugar
175g/6oz/1½ cups plain flour
30ml/2 tbsp fresh lavender florets or 15ml/1 tbsp dried culinary lavender, roughly chopped
30ml/2 tbsp superfine sugar for sprinkling

1 Cream together the butter and sugar until fluffy. Stir in the flour and lavender and bring the mixture together in a soft ball. Cover and chill for 15 minutes.

2 Preheat the oven to 200°C/400°F/Gas 6. Roll out the dough on a lightly floured surface and stamp out about 18 biscuits, using a 5cm/2in heart-shaped cutter. Place on a heavy baking sheet and bake for about 10 minutes, until golden.

3 Leave the biscuits standing for 5 minutes to set. Using a metal spatula, transfer carefully from the baking sheet on to a wire rack to cool completely. The biscuits can be stored in an airtight container for up to one week.

Vanilla Crescents

These attractively shaped cookies are sweet and delicate, ideal for an elegant afternoon tea.

Makes 36

INGREDIENTS

175g/6oz/1¼ cups unblanched almonds
115g/4oz/1 cup plain flour
pinch of salt
225g/8oz/1 cup unsalted butter
115g/4oz/½ cup granulated sugar
5ml/1 tsp vanilla essence
icing sugar for dusting

1 Grind the almonds with a few tablespoons of the flour in a food processor, blender or nut grinder.

2 Sift the remaining flour with the salt into a bowl. Set aside.

3 With an electric mixer, cream together the butter and sugar until light and fluffy.

4 Add the almonds, vanilla essence and the flour mixture. Stir to mix well. Gather the dough into a ball, wrap in greaseproof paper, and chill for at least 30 minutes.

5 Preheat the oven to 160°C/325°F/Gas 3. Lightly grease two baking sheets.

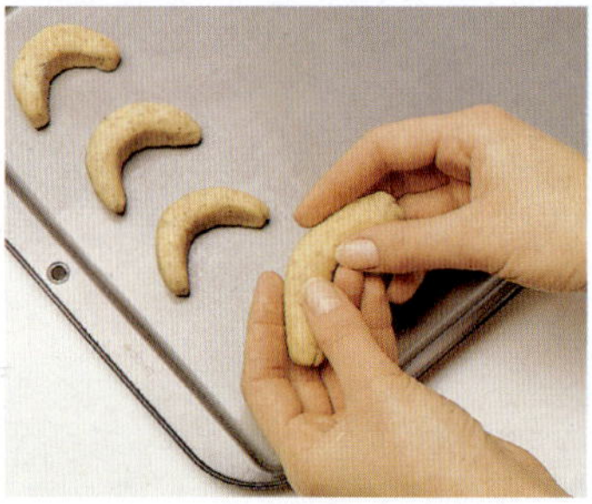

6 Break off walnut-size pieces of dough and roll into small cylinders about 1cm/½in in diameter. Bend into small crescents and place on the prepared baking sheets.

7 Bake for about 20 minutes until dry but not brown. Transfer to a wire rack to cool only slightly. Set the rack over a baking sheet and dust with an even layer of icing sugar. Leave to cool completely.

Mexican Aniseed Cookies

Makes 24

INGREDIENTS

175g/6oz/1½ cups plain flour
5ml/1 tsp baking powder
pinch of salt
115g/4oz/½ cup unsalted butter
115g/4oz/½ cup caster sugar
1 egg
5ml/1 tsp whole aniseed
15ml/1 tbsp brandy
50g/2oz/¼ cup caster sugar mixed with 2.5ml/½ tsp ground cinnamon for sprinkling

1 Sift together the flour, baking powder and salt. Set aside.

2 Beat the butter with the sugar until soft and fluffy. Add the egg, aniseed and brandy and beat until incorporated. Fold in the dry ingredients until just blended to a dough. Chill for 30 minutes.

3 Preheat the oven to 180°C/350°F/Gas 4. Grease two baking sheets.

4 On a lightly floured surface, roll out the chilled dough to about 3mm/⅛in thick.

5 With a floured cutter, pastry wheel or knife, cut out the biscuits into squares, diamonds or other shapes. The traditional shape for biscochitos is a fleur-de-lis but you might find this a bit too ambitious.

6 Place on the prepared baking sheets and sprinkle lightly with the cinnamon sugar.

7 Bake for about 10 minutes, until just barely golden. Cool on the baking sheet for 5 minutes before transferring to a wire rack to cool completely. The biscuits can be kept in an airtight container for up to one week.

Festive and Fancy Cookies

Over the years, some cookies have become associated with certain festivals – Jewelled Christmas Trees dangle jauntily from the tree at Christmas, Easter Cookies always find their way into the cookie jar at that time of the year, and at carnival time Italians would feel deprived if Italian Pastry Twists did not make an appearance. Other cookies are festive just because they are fancy. Chocolate-dipped Hazelnut Crescents or Black-and-White Ginger Florentines immediately perk up the spirits and make you feel something special is happening.

If you are making cookies for a holiday period such as school holidays, try to select recipes that keep well so you can make them a week or so in advance. Alternatively, freeze them, either raw or baked. Don't forget to make a note of how long they need to thaw, plus the baking time for raw cookies, and remember that cooked ones will benefit from being refreshed in the oven.

Baklava

This, the queen of all pastries, is enjoyed all year but is specially associated with the Persian New Year on 21st March, celebrating the first day of spring.

Makes 30

INGREDIENTS

350g/12oz/3 cups ground pistachios
150g/5oz/1¼ cups icing sugar
15ml/1 tbsp ground cardamom
150g/5oz/⅔ cup unsalted butter, melted
450g/1lb filo pastry
For the syrup
450g/1lb/2 cups granulated sugar
300ml/½ pint/1¼ cups water
30ml/2 tbsp rosewater

1 Place the sugar and water in a saucepan, bring to the boil and simmer for 10 minutes, until syrupy. Stir in the rosewater. Mix together the nuts, icing sugar and cardamom. Preheat the oven to 160°C/325°F/Gas 3. Brush a baking tin with butter.

2 Taking one sheet of filo pastry at a time, and keeping the remainder covered with a damp cloth, brush with melted butter and lay on the bottom of the tin. Continue until you have six buttered layers in the tin. Spread half of the nut mixture over, pressing down with a spoon.

3 Take another six sheets of filo pastry, brush with butter and lay over the nut mixture. Sprinkle over the remaining nuts and top with a final layer of six filo sheets. Cut the pastry into small lozenge shapes. Pour the remaining butter over the top. Bake for 20 minutes then increase the heat to 200°C/400°F/Gas 6 and bake for 15 minutes, until light golden in colour and puffed.

4 Remove from the oven and drizzle most of the syrup over the pastry, reserving the remainder for serving.

Cinnamon Balls

These almond balls should be soft inside, with a very strong cinnamon flavour. They harden with keeping, so it is a good idea to freeze some and only use them when required.

Makes 15

INGREDIENTS

175g/6oz/1½ cups ground almonds
75g/3oz/⅓ cup caster sugar
15ml/1 tbsp ground cinnamon
2 egg whites
oil for greasing
icing sugar for dredging

1 Preheat the oven to 180°C/350°F/Gas 4. Oil a large baking sheet. Mix together the ground almonds, sugar and cinnamon. Whisk the egg whites until they begin to stiffen and fold enough into the almonds to make a fairly firm mixture.

2 Wet your hands with cold water and roll small spoonfuls of the mixture into balls. Place these on the prepared baking sheet.

3 Bake for about 15 minutes, so they remain slightly soft inside – too much cooking will make them hard and tough. Slide a palette knife under the balls to release them from the baking sheet and leave to cool.

4 Sift a few tablespoons of icing sugar on to a plate. When the cinnamon balls are cold slide them on to the plate. Shake gently to completely cover the cinnamon balls in sugar. Store in an airtight container or in the freezer.

Coconut Pyramids

Coconut biscuits are sold in Israeli street markets during Passover.

Makes 15

INGREDIENTS

225g/8oz/1 cup desiccated coconut
115g/4oz/½ cup caster sugar
2 egg whites

Cook's Tip The heat in ovens tends to be uneven, so, if necessary, turn the sheets round during baking for the pyramids to brown evenly.

1 Preheat the oven to 190°C/375°F/Gas 5. Grease a large baking sheet with a little oil.

2 Mix together the desiccated coconut and sugar. Lightly whisk the egg whites. Fold enough egg white into the coconut to make a fairly firm mixture. You may not need quite all the egg whites.

3 Form the mixture into pyramid shapes by taking a teaspoonful and rolling it first into a ball. Flatten the base and press the top into a point. Arrange the pyramids on the prepared baking sheet.

4 Bake for 12–15 minutes on a low shelf. The tips should begin to turn golden and the pyramids should be just firm, but still soft inside.

5 Slide a palette knife under the pyramids and leave to cool before transferring to a wire rack.

Easter Cookies

These are enjoyed as a traditional part of the Christian festival of Easter.

Makes 16–18

INGREDIENTS

115g/4oz/½ cup butter, chopped
75g/3oz/⅓ cup caster sugar, plus extra for sprinkling
1 egg, separated
200g/7oz/1¾ cups plain four
2.5ml/½ tsp ground mixed spice
2.5ml/½ tsp ground cinnamon
50g/2oz/scant ⅓ cup currants
15ml/1 tbsp chopped mixed peel
15–30ml/1–2 tbsp milk

1 Preheat the oven to 200°C/400°F/Gas 6. Lightly grease two baking sheets. Beat together the butter and sugar, then beat in the egg yolk.

2 Sift the flour and spices over the egg mixture, then fold in with the currants and peel, adding sufficient milk to mix to a fairly soft dough.

3 Turn the dough on to a floured surface, knead lightly until just smooth, then roll out using a floured rolling pin, to about 5mm/¼in thick. Cut the dough into rounds using a 5cm/2in fluted biscuit cutter. Transfer the rounds to the prepared baking sheets and bake for 10 minutes.

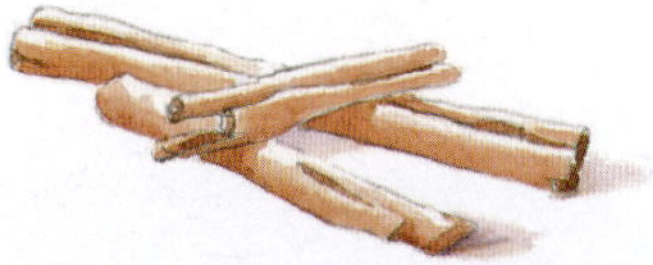

4 Beat the egg white, then brush over the biscuits. Sprinkle with caster sugar and return to the oven for a further 10 minutes, until golden. Transfer to a wire rack to cool.

Italian Pastry Twists

Deep-fried pastry twists, hearts or knots, traditionally flavoured with vin santo, *a sherry-like Italian wine, are served hot, dusted with icing sugar, at Italian carnival time.*

Makes 40

INGREDIENTS

250g/9oz/2¼ cups plain flour
1 egg
pinch of salt
25g/1oz/2 tbsp granulated sugar
2.5ml/½ tsp vanilla essence
25g/1oz/2 tbsp butter, melted
45–60ml/3–4 tbsp sherry
oil for deep-frying
icing sugar for sprinkling

1 Sift the flour into a large mixing bowl and make a well in the centre. Add the egg, salt, sugar, vanilla essence and melted butter.

2 Mix with your hands until the mixture starts to come together. When the dough becomes stiff, add enough sherry to make the dough soft and pliable. Knead until smooth and then wrap and chill for about 1 hour.

3 Roll out the pastry thinly and cut into 40 18 x 1cm/7 x ½in strips. Tie each strip loosely into a knot.

4 Heat the oil in a pan to 190°C/375°F and deep-fry the knots in batches for 2–3 minutes, until puffed up and golden.

5 Drain the pastry twists on kitchen paper, sprinkle generously with icing sugar and serve either hot or cold with coffee.

Apricot Meringue Bars

Makes 16

INGREDIENTS

50g/2oz/½ cup plain flour
50g/2oz/½ cup butter
2.5ml/½ tsp vanilla essence
large pinch of salt
1 large egg, separated
115g/4oz/½ cup caster sugar
50g/2oz/⅓ cup chopped walnuts
50g/2oz/⅓ cup chopped pecans
115g/4oz/½ cup apricot jam

1 Preheat the oven to 180°C/350°F/Gas 4. Grease a 20cm/9in square baking tin. Beat together the flour, butter, vanilla essence, salt, egg yolk and 50g/2oz/¼ cup of the sugar. Spread the mixture evenly over the base of the baking tin, prick it all over with a fork and bake in the oven for 10 minutes.

2 Beat the egg white until stiff. Gradually beat in the remaining 50g/2oz/¼ cup sugar until the mixture is smooth and glossy. Gently fold in the chopped walnuts and pecans, but do not over-mix.

3 Remove the tin from the oven, spread the apricot jam over the base and spread the meringue mixture to cover it evenly.

4 Bake in the oven for 20 minutes, until the meringue is crisp and light brown. Cool on a wire rack, then cut into 10 x 2.5cm/4 x 1in bars for serving.

Cook's Tip Apricot Meringue Bars may be stored in an airtight container for up to 3 days.

Moravian Tarts

Makes 35

INGREDIENTS

115g/4oz/½ cup unsalted butter
2.5ml/½ tsp vanilla essence
large pinch of salt
150g/5oz/scant ⅔ cup caster sugar
1 egg, beaten
115g/4oz/1 cup plain flour
1.5ml/¼ tsp bicarbonate of soda
7.5ml/1½ tsp ground cinnamon
1 egg white, lightly beaten
35 pecan halves

1 Cream the butter, vanilla essence, salt and 115g/4oz/½ cup of the sugar until light and fluffy. Gradually add the egg, beating constantly.

2 Sift together the flour, bicarbonate of soda and 2.5ml/½ tsp of the cinnamon and stir a little at a time into the butter mixture. Form the mixture into a dough and chill overnight. Remove from the refrigerator 30 minutes before using.

3 Preheat the oven to 180°C/350°F/Gas 4. Lightly grease a baking sheet. Roll out the dough until it is about 3mm/⅛in thick. Cut into rounds with a 5cm/2in cutter.

4 Place the rounds on the prepared baking sheet and brush the tops with the egg white. Mix the remaining ground cinnamon with the remaining caster sugar. Sprinkle over the rounds and press a pecan half into each centre. Bake for 8–10 minutes, until golden brown.

Glazed Ginger Cookies

These also make good hanging biscuits for decorating trees and garlands. For this, make a hole in each biscuit with a skewer, and thread with fine ribbon.

Makes about 20

INGREDIENTS

1 quantity Golden Gingerbread mixture
2 quantities Icing Glaze
red and green food colourings
175g/6oz white almond paste

1 Preheat the oven to 180°C/350°F/Gas 4. Grease a large baking sheet. Roll out the gingerbread dough on a floured surface and, using a selection of floured cookie cutters, cut out a variety of shapes, such as trees, stars, crescents and bells. Transfer to the prepared baking sheet and bake for 8–10 minutes, until just beginning to colour around the edges. Leave the cookies on the baking sheet for 3 minutes.

2 Transfer the cookies to a wire rack and leave to cool. Place the wire rack over a large tray or plate. Using a dessertspoon, spoon the icing glaze over the cookies until they are completely covered. Leave in a cool place to dry for several hours.

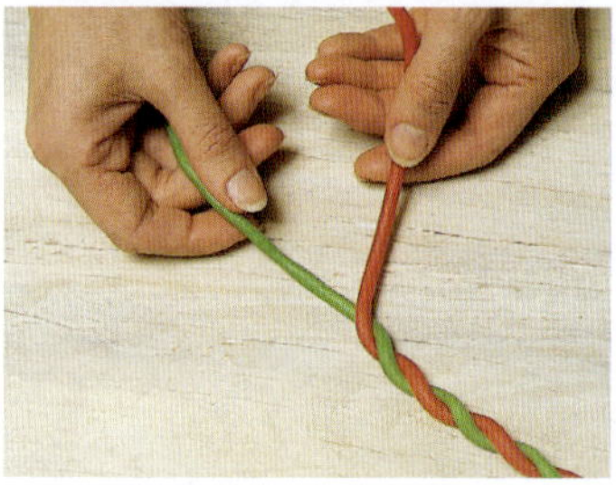

3 Knead red food colouring into half of the almond paste and green into the other half. Roll a thin length of each coloured paste and then twist the two together into a rope.

4 Secure a rope of paste around a biscuit, dampening the icing with a little water, if necessary, to hold it in place. Repeat on about half of the cookies. Dilute a little of each food colouring with water. Using a fine paintbrush, paint festive decorations over the plain cookies. Leave to dry and then wrap in tissue paper.

Christmas Cookies

Makes 30

INGREDIENTS

175g/6oz/¾ cup unsalted butter
300g/11oz/1¼ cups caster sugar
1 egg
1 egg yolk
5ml/1 tsp vanilla essence
grated rind of 1 lemon
pinch of salt
300g/11oz/2½ cups plain flour
For the decoration (optional)
coloured icing and small sweets such as silver balls, coloured sugar crystals

1 With an electric mixer, cream the butter until soft. Add the sugar gradually and continue beating until light and fluffy.

2 Using a wooden spoon, slowly mix in the whole egg and the egg yolk. Add the vanilla essence, lemon rind and salt. Stir to mix well.

3 Sift the flour over the mixture and stir to blend. Gather the dough into a ball, wrap, and chill for 30 minutes.

4 Preheat the oven to 190°C/375°F/Gas 5. On a floured surface, roll out until about 3mm/⅛in thick.

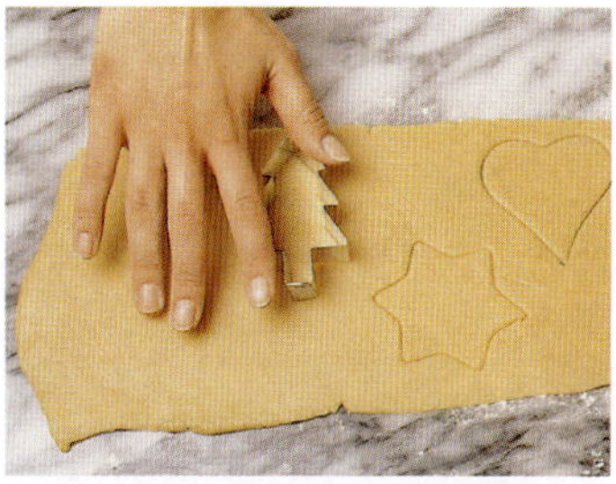

5 Stamp out shapes or rounds with floured cookie cutters.

6 Bake for about 8 minutes until lightly coloured. Transfer to a wire rack and leave to cool completely before decorating, if wished, with icing and sweets.

Jewelled Christmas Trees

These cookies make an appealing gift. They look wonderful hung on a Christmas tree or in front of a window to catch the light.

Makes 12

INGREDIENTS

175g/6oz/1½ cups plain flour
75g/3oz/⅓ cup butter, chopped
40g/1½oz/3 tbsp caster sugar
1 egg white
30ml/2 tbsp orange juice
225g/8oz coloured fruit sweets
coloured ribbons, to decorate

1 Preheat the oven to 180°C/350°F/Gas 4. Line two baking sheets with non-stick baking paper. Sift the flour into a mixing bowl.

2 Rub the butter into the flour until the mixture resembles fine breadcrumbs. Stir in the sugar, egg white and enough orange juice to form a soft dough. Knead on a lightly floured surface until smooth.

3 Roll out thinly and stamp out as many shapes as possible using a floured Christmas tree cutter. Transfer the shapes to the prepared baking sheets, spacing them well apart. Knead the trimmings together.

4 Using a 1cm/½in round cutter or the end of a large plain piping nozzle, stamp out and remove six rounds from each tree shape. Cut each sweet into three and place a piece in each hole. Make a small hole at the top of each tree to thread through the ribbon.

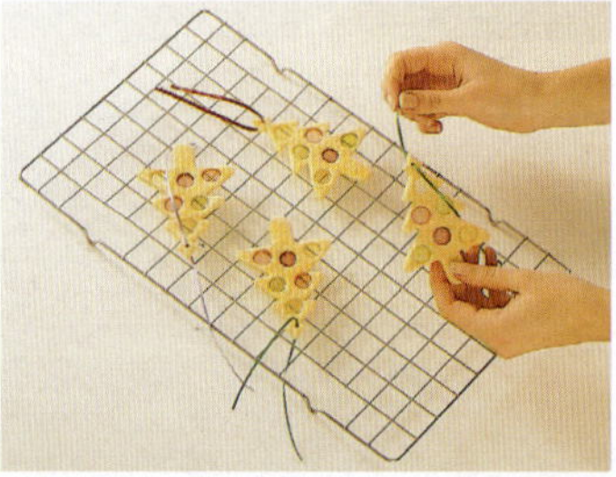

5 Bake for 15–20 minutes, until the biscuits are slightly gold in colour and the sweets have melted and filled the holes. Cool on the baking sheets. Repeat until you have used up the remaining cookie dough and sweets. Thread short lengths of ribbon through the holes so that the biscuits can be hung up.

Cranberry and Chocolate Squares

Made for each other – that's the contrasting flavours of tangy-sharp cranberries and sweet chocolate.

Makes 12

INGREDIENTS

115g/4oz/½ cup unsalted butter
60ml/4 tbsp cocoa powder
215g/7½oz/1¼ cups light muscovado sugar
150g/5oz/1¼ cups self-raising flour
2 eggs, beaten
115g/4oz/1 cup fresh or thawed frozen cranberries
For the topping
150ml/¼ pint/⅔ cup soured cream
75g/3oz/6 tbsp caster sugar
30ml/2 tbsp self-raising flour
50g/2oz/4 tbsp soft margarine
1 egg, beaten
2.5ml/½ tsp vanilla essence
75ml/5 tbsp coarsely grated plain chocolate for sprinkling

1 Preheat the oven to 180°C/350°F/Gas 4. Grease an 18 x 25cm/7 x 10in cake tin and dust lightly with flour. Combine the butter, cocoa and sugar in a saucepan and stir over a low heat until melted and smooth.

2 Remove from the heat and stir in the flour and eggs. Stir in the cranberries, then spread the mixture in the prepared cake tin.

3 To make the topping, mix all the ingredients, except the chocolate, in a bowl. Beat until smooth, then spread over the base.

4 Sprinkle with the grated chocolate and bake for 40–45 minutes, until risen and firm. Cool in the tin, then cut into 12 squares.

Biscotti

These lovely Italian biscuits are part-baked, sliced to reveal a feast of mixed nuts and then baked again until crisp and golden. Traditionally they're served dipped in vin santo, *a sweet dessert wine.*

Makes 24

INGREDIENTS

50g/2oz/¼ cup unsalted butter
115g/4oz/½ cup caster sugar
175g/6oz/1½ cups self-raising flour
pinch of salt
10ml/2 tsp baking powder
5ml/1 tsp ground coriander
finely grated rind of 1 lemon
50g/2oz/½ cup polenta
1 egg, lightly beaten
10ml/2 tsp brandy or orange-flavoured liqueur
50g/2oz/½ cup unblanched almonds
50g/2oz/½ cup pistachios

1 Preheat the oven to 160°C/325°F/Gas 3. Lightly grease a baking sheet. Cream together the butter and sugar in a bowl.

2 Sift the flour, salt, baking powder and coriander into the bowl. Add the lemon rind, polenta, egg and brandy or liqueur and mix together to make a soft dough.

3 Stir in the nuts until evenly combined. Halve the mixture. Shape each half into a flat sausage about 23cm/9in long and 6cm/2½in wide. Bake for about 30 minutes, until risen and firm. Remove from the oven.

4 When cool, cut each sausage diagonally into 12 thin slices. Return to the baking sheet and cook for a further 10 minutes, until crisp.

5 Transfer to a wire rack to cool completely. Store in an airtight container for up to one week.

Cook's Tip Use a sharp, serrated knife to slice the cooled biscuits, otherwise they will crumble.

Sultana Cornmeal Cookies

These little yellow biscuits come from the Veneto region of Italy.

Makes 48

INGREDIENTS

75g/3oz/½ cup sultanas
115g/4oz/1 cup finely ground yellow cornmeal
175g/6oz/1½ cups plain flour
7.5ml/1½ tsp baking powder
pinch of salt
225g/8oz/1 cup butter
225g/8oz/1 cup granulated sugar
2 eggs
15ml/1 tbsp marsala or 5ml/1 tsp vanilla essence

1 Soak the sultanas in a small bowl of warm water for 15 minutes. Drain. Preheat the oven to 180°C/350°F/Gas 4. Grease a baking sheet.

2 Sift the cornmeal, flour, baking powder and salt together into a mixing bowl. Set aside.

3 Cream the butter and sugar until light and fluffy. Beat in the eggs, one at a time. Beat in the marsala or vanilla essence.

4 Add the dry ingredients to the butter mixture, beating until well blended. Stir in the sultanas.

5 Drop heaped teaspoons of the mixture on to the prepared baking sheet in rows about 5cm/2in apart. Bake for 7–8 minutes, until the cookies are golden brown at the edges. Transfer to a wire rack to cool.

Amaretti

If bitter almonds are not available, make up the weight with sweet almonds.

Makes 36

INGREDIENTS

150g/5oz/1¼ cups sweet almonds
50g/2oz/½ cup bitter almonds
225g/8oz/1 cup caster sugar
2 egg whites
2.5ml/½ tsp almond essence or 5ml/1 tsp vanilla essence
icing sugar for dusting

1 Preheat the oven to 160°C/325°F/Gas 3. Peel the almonds by dropping them into a saucepan of boiling water for 1–2 minutes. Drain. Rub the almonds in a cloth to remove the skins.

2 Place the almonds on a baking tray and let them dry out in the oven for 10–15 minutes without browning. Remove from the oven and allow to cool. Turn the oven off. Dust with flour.

3 Grind the almonds with half of the sugar in a food processor. Use an electric beater or wire whisk to beat the egg whites until they form soft peaks.

4 Sprinkle over half the remaining sugar and continue beating until stiff peaks are formed. Gently fold in the remaining sugar, the almond or vanilla essence and the almonds.

5 Spoon the almond mixture into a piping bag fitted with a smooth nozzle. Pipe out the mixture in rounds the size of a walnut. Sprinkle lightly with the icing sugar, and leave to stand for 2 hours. Near the end of this time, turn the oven on again and preheat to 180°C/350°F/Gas 4.

6 Bake for 15 minutes, until pale gold. Remove from the oven and cool on a wire rack.

Macaroons

Freshly ground almonds, lightly toasted beforehand to intensify the flavour, give these biscuits their rich taste and texture so, for best results, avoid using ready-ground almonds as a shortcut.

Makes 12

INGREDIENTS

115g/4oz/1½ cup blanched almonds, toasted
165g/5½oz/¾ cup caster sugar
2 egg whites
2.5ml/½ tsp almond or vanilla essence
icing sugar for dusting

1 Preheat the oven to 180°C/350°F/Gas 4. Line a large baking sheet with non-stick baking paper. Reserve 12 almonds for decorating. In a food processor grind the rest of the almonds with the sugar.

2 With the machine running, slowly pour in enough of the egg whites to form a soft dough. Add the almond or vanilla essence and pulse to mix.

3 With moistened hands, shape the mixture into walnut-size balls and arrange on the baking sheet.

4 Press one of the reserved almonds on to each ball, flattening them slightly, and dust lightly with icing sugar. Bake for about 10–12 minutes, until the tops are golden and feel slightly firm. Transfer to a wire rack, cool slightly, then peel the biscuits off the paper and leave to cool completely.

Cook's Tip To toast the almonds, spread them on a baking sheet and bake in the preheated oven for 10–15 minutes, until golden. Leave to cool before grinding.

Madeleines

These little tea cakes, baked in a special tin with shell-shaped cups, were made famous by Marcel Proust, who referred to them in his novel. They are best eaten on the day they are made.

Makes 12

INGREDIENTS

165g/5½oz/1¼ cups plain flour
5ml/1 tsp baking powder
2 eggs
75g/3oz/¾ cup icing sugar, plus extra for dusting
grated rind of 1 lemon or orange
15ml/1 tbsp lemon or orange juice
75g/3oz/6 tbsp unsalted butter, melted and slightly cooled

1 Preheat the oven to 190°C/375°F/Gas 5. Generously butter a 12-cup madeleine tin. Sift together the flour and baking powder.

2 Using an electric mixer, beat the eggs and icing sugar for 5–7 minutes until thick and creamy and the mixture forms a ribbon when the beaters are lifted. Gently fold in the lemon or orange rind and juice.

3 Beginning with the flour mixture, alternately fold in the flour and melted butter in four batches. Leave the mixture to stand for 10 minutes, then carefully spoon into the tin. Tap gently to release any air bubbles.

4 Bake for 12–15 minutes, rotating the tin halfway through cooking, until a skewer or cake tester inserted in the centre comes out clean. Tip on to a wire rack to cool completely and dust with icing sugar before serving.

Cook's Tip If you don't have a special tin for making madeleines, you can use a bun tin, preferably with a non-stick coating. The cakes won't have the characteristic ridges and shell shape, but they are quite pretty dusted with a little icing sugar.

Chocolate Macaroons

Makes 20

INGREDIENTS

50g/2oz plain chocolate chopped into small pieces
115g/4oz/1 cup blanched almonds
2 egg whites
200g/7oz/1 cup caster sugar
2.5ml/½ tsp vanilla essence
1.5ml/¼ tsp almond essence
icing sugar for dusting

1 Preheat the oven to 150°C/300°F/ Gas 2. Line two baking sheets with non-stick baking paper.

2 Melt the chocolate in the top of a double boiler, or in a heatproof bowl placed over a saucepan of barely simmering water.

3 Grind the almonds finely in a food processor, blender or nut grinder.

4 In a mixing bowl, whisk the egg whites until they form soft peaks. Fold in the sugar, vanilla and almond essence, ground almonds and cooled melted chocolate. The mixture should just hold its shape. If it is too soft, chill it in the fridge for 15 minutes.

5 Place heaped teaspoonfuls of the mixture, spaced well apart, on the prepared baking sheets and flatten slightly. Brush each ball with a little water and sift over a thin layer of icing sugar.

6 Bake for 20-25 minutes until just firm. With a metal spatula, transfer to a wire rack and allow to cool completely.

Variation For Chocolate Pine Nut Macaroons, spread 75g/3oz/¾ cup pine nuts in a shallow dish. Press the balls of chocolate macaroon dough into the nuts to cover one side and bake as described, nut-side up.

Coconut Macaroons

Makes 24

INGREDIENTS

40g/1½oz/⅓ cup plain flour
pinch of salt
215g/7½oz/2½ cups desiccated coconut
150ml/¼ pint/⅔ cup sweetened condensed milk
5ml/1 tsp vanilla essence

1 Preheat the oven to 180°C/350°F/ Gas 4. Line two baking sheets with greaseproof paper and grease the paper.

2 Sift the flour and salt into a large bowl. Stir in the dessicated coconut.

3 Pour in the sweetened condensed milk. Add the vanilla essence and stir together from the centre. Continue stirring until a very thick batter is formed.

4 Drop heaped tablespoonfuls of batter 2.5cm/1in apart on the prepared baking sheets. Bake the macaroons for about 20 minutes, until golden brown. Transfer to a wire rack to cool.

Variation For a very rich, sweet and tempting *petits four*, make the macaroons smaller, and when cooked coat them in melted plain chocolate. Place on greaseproof paper and leave until the chocolate is hard. Serve with small cups of strong, black coffee after a dinner party.

Brandy Snaps

Eat these on high days and holidays as an indulgent treat.

Makes 18

INGREDIENTS

50g/2oz/4 tbsp butter
150g/5oz/⅔ cup caster sugar
7.5ml/1 rounded tbsp golden syrup
40g/1½oz/⅓ cup plain flour
2.5ml/½ tsp ground ginger
For the filling
250ml/8fl oz/1 cup whipping cream
30ml/2 tbsp brandy

1 With an electric mixer, cream together the butter and sugar until light and fluffy, then beat in the golden syrup. Sift over the flour and ginger and mix to a rough dough.

2 Transfer the dough to a work surface and knead until smooth. Cover and chill for 30 minutes.

3 Preheat the oven to 190°C/375°F/ Gas 5. Grease a baking sheet.

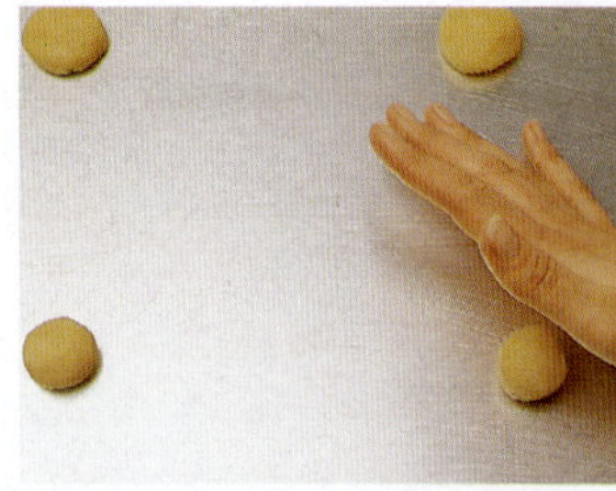

4 Working in batches of four, form walnut-size balls of dough. Place well apart on the prepared baking sheet and flatten slightly. Bake for about 10 minutes, until golden.

5 Remove from the oven and leave to cool for a few moments. Working quickly, slide a metal spatula under each biscuit, turn over, and wrap around the handle of a wooden spoon. When firm, slide off the snaps and place on a wire rack to cool.

6 To make the filling, whip the cream and brandy until soft peaks form. Fill a piping bag and pipe into each end of the brandy snaps just before serving.

Chocolate-dipped Hazelnut Crescents

Walnuts or pecans can be used instead of hazelnuts, but they must be finely ground.

Makes 35

INGREDIENTS

300g/11oz/2½ cups plain flour
pinch of salt
225g/8oz/1 cup unsalted butter
50g/2oz/¼ cup caster sugar
15ml/1 tbsp hazelnut liqueur or water
5ml/1 tsp vanilla essence
75g/3oz plain chocolate, finely grated
65g/2½oz/½ cup hazelnuts, toasted and finely chopped
icing sugar for dusting
350g/12oz plain chocolate, melted, for dipping

1 Preheat the oven to 160°C/325°F/Gas 3. Grease two large baking sheets. Sift the flour and salt into a small bowl.

2 In a large bowl, using an electric mixer, beat the butter until creamy. Add the sugar and beat until fluffy, beat in the hazelnut liqueur or water and vanilla essence. Gently stir in the flour, until just blended, then fold in the grated chocolate and hazelnuts.

3 With floured hands, shape the dough into 5 x 1cm/2 x ½in crescent shapes. Place on the prepared baking sheets, 5cm/2in apart. Bake for 20–25 minutes, until the edges are set and the cookies slightly golden. Remove the baking sheets to a wire rack to cool for 10 minutes. Transfer the biscuits from the baking sheets to wire racks to cool completely.

4 Line the baking sheets with non-stick baking paper. Dust the cookies with icing sugar. Using a pair of kitchen tongs, or fingers, dip half of each crescent into melted chocolate. Place on the prepared baking sheets. Chill until the chocolate has set.

Black-and-White Ginger Florentines

These florentines can be refrigerated in an airtight container for one week.

Makes 30

INGREDIENTS

120ml/4fl oz/½ cup double cream
50g/2oz/¼ cup unsalted butter
90g/3½oz/½ cup granulated sugar
30ml/2 tbsp honey
150g/5oz/1⅓ cups flaked almonds
40g/1½oz/⅓ cup plain flour
2.5ml/½ tsp ground ginger
50g/2oz/⅓ cup diced candied orange peel
65g/2½oz/½ cup diced stem ginger
200g/7oz plain chocolate, chopped
150g/5oz fine quality white chocolate, chopped

1 Preheat the oven to 180°C/350°F/Gas 4. Lightly grease two large baking sheets. In a medium saucepan over a medium heat, stir the cream, butter, sugar and honey until the sugar dissolves. Bring the mixture to the boil, stirring constantly.

2 Remove from the heat and stir in the almonds, flour and ground ginger until well blended. Stir in the orange peel, stem ginger and 50g/2oz/⅓ cup chopped plain chocolate.

3 Drop teaspoons of the mixture on to the prepared baking sheets at least 7.5cm/3in apart. Spread each round as thinly as possible with the back of the spoon. (Dip the spoon in water to prevent sticking.)

4 Bake in batches for 8–10 minutes, until the edges are golden brown and the biscuits are bubbling. Do not under-bake or they will be sticky, but be careful not to over-bake as they burn easily. If you wish, use a 7.5cm/3in biscuit cutter to neaten the edges of the florentines while on the baking sheet.

5 Remove the baking sheet to the wire rack to cool for 10 minutes until firm. Using a metal palette knife, carefully transfer the florentines to a wire rack to cool completely.

6 In a small saucepan over a very low heat, melt the remaining chocolate, stirring frequently, until smooth. Cool slightly. In the top of a double boiler over a low heat, melt the white chocolate until smooth, stirring frequently. Remove the top of double boiler from the bottom and cool for about 5 minutes, stirring occasionally until slightly thickened.

7 Using a small metal palette knife, spread half the florentines with the plain chocolate on the flat side of each biscuit, swirling to create a decorative surface, and place on a wire rack, chocolate side up. Spread the remaining florentines with the melted white chocolate and place on the rack, chocolate side up. Chill for 10–15 minutes to set completely.

Tuiles d'Amandes

These biscuits are named after the French roof tiles they so resemble. Making them is a little fiddly, so bake only four at a time until you get the knack. With a little practice you will find them easy.

Makes 24

INGREDIENTS

65g/2½oz/generous ½ cup whole blanched almonds, lightly toasted
65g/2½oz/⅓ cup caster sugar
40g/1½oz/3 tbsp unsalted butter
2 egg whites
2.5ml/½ tsp almond essence
30g/1¼oz/scant ¼ cup plain flour, sifted
50g/2oz/½ cup flaked almonds

Cook's Tip If the biscuits flatten or lose their crispness, reheat them on a baking sheet in a moderate oven, until completely flat, then reshape.

1 Preheat the oven to 200°C/400°F/Gas 6. Generously butter two heavy baking sheets.

2 Place the almonds and about 30ml/2 tbsp of the sugar in a food processor fitted with the metal blade and process until finely ground.

3 Beat the butter until creamy, then add the remaining sugar and beat until light and fluffy. Gradually beat in the egg whites, then add the almond essence. Sift the flour over the butter mixture, fold in, then fold in the ground almond mixture.

4 Drop tablespoonfuls of the mixture on to the prepared baking sheets about 15cm/6in apart. With the back of a wet spoon, spread each mound into a paper-thin 7.5cm/3in round. (Don't worry if holes appear, they will fill in.) Sprinkle with flaked almonds.

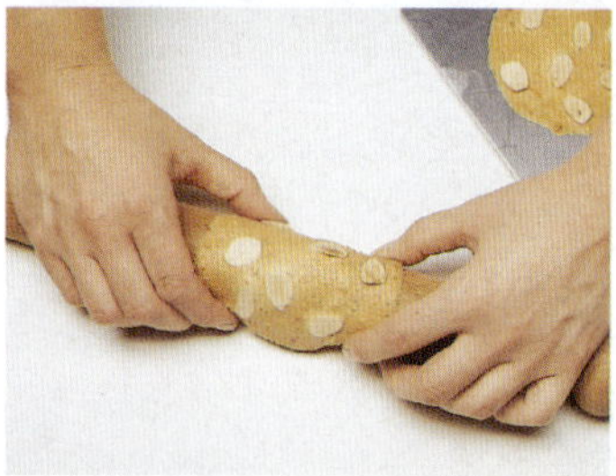

5 Bake the cookies, one sheet at a time, for 5–6 minutes, until the edges are golden and the centres still pale. Working quickly, use a thin palette knife to loosen the edges of one cookie. Lift the cookie on the palette knife and place over a rolling pin, then press down the sides of the biscuit to curve it.

6 Continue shaping the cookies, transferring them to a wire rack as they cool. If they become too crisp to shape, return the baking sheet to the hot oven for 15–30 seconds, then continue as above.

Flaked Almond Biscuits

Makes 30

INGREDIENTS

175g/6oz/¾ cup butter or margarine, chopped
225g/8oz/2 cups self-raising flour
150g/5oz/⅔ cup caster sugar
2.5ml/½ tsp ground cinnamon
1 egg, separated
30ml/2 tbsp cold water
50g/2oz/½ cup flaked almonds

1 Preheat the oven to 180°C/350°F/Gas 4. Rub the butter or margarine into the flour. Reserve 15ml/1 tbsp of the sugar and mix the rest with the cinnamon. Stir into the flour and then add the egg yolk and cold water and mix to a firm dough.

2 Roll out the dough on a lightly floured board to 1cm/½in thick. Sprinkle over the almonds. Continue rolling until the dough is approximately 5mm/¼in thick.

3 Using a floured fluted round cutter, cut the dough into rounds. Use a palette knife to lift them on to an ungreased baking sheet. Re-form the dough and cut more rounds to use all the dough. Whisk the egg white lightly, brush it over the cookies, and sprinkle over the remaining sugar.

4 Bake for about 10–15 minutes, until golden. To remove, slide a palette knife under the cookies, which will still seem a bit soft, but they harden as they cool. Leave on a wire rack until quite cold.

Nut Lace Cookies

Makes 18

INGREDIENTS

50g/2oz/½ cup blanched almonds
50g/2oz/4 tbsp butter
45ml/3 tbsp plain flour
115g/4oz/½ cup granulated sugar
30ml/2 tbsp double cream
2.5ml/½ tsp vanilla essence

Variation Add 40g/1½oz/¼ cup finely chopped candied orange peel to the mixture.

1 Preheat the oven to 190°C/375°F/Gas 5. Grease 1–2 baking sheets.

2 With a sharp knife, chop the almonds as finely as possible. Alternatively, use a food processor, blender or nut grinder to chop the nuts very finely.

3 Melt the butter in a small saucepan over a low heat. Remove from the heat and stir in the remaining ingredients, including the almonds.

4 Drop teaspoonfuls of the mixture 6cm/2½in apart on the prepared baking sheets. Bake for about 5 minutes until golden. Cool on the sheets briefly, until the cookies are just stiff enough to lift off.

5 With a metal spatula, transfer the cookies to a wire rack to cool completely.

Oatmeal Lace Cookies

Makes 36

INGREDIENTS

165g/5½oz/⅔ cup butter or margarine
175g/6oz/1½ cups rolled oats
175g/6oz/¾ cup firmly packed dark brown sugar
175g/6oz/¾ cup granulated sugar
45ml/3 tbsp plain flour
pinch of salt
1 egg, lightly beaten
5ml/1 tsp vanilla essence
50g/2oz/½ cup pecans or walnuts, finely chopped

1 Preheat the oven to 180°C/350°F/Gas 4. Grease two baking sheets.

2 Melt the butter or margarine in a small saucepan over a low heat. Set aside.

3 In a mixing bowl, combine the oats, brown sugar, granulated sugar, flour and salt.

4 Add the butter or margarine, the egg and vanilla essence.

5 Mix until blended, then stir in the chopped nuts.

6 Drop rounded teaspoonfuls of the batter about 5cm/2in apart on the prepared baking sheets. Bake for 5–8 minutes until lightly browned on the edges and bubbling. Leave to cool for 2 minutes, then transfer to a wire rack to cool completely.

Strawberry Shortcakes

A favourite American summer dessert.

Makes 6

INGREDIENTS

450g/1lb strawberries, hulled and halved or quartered, depending on size
45ml/3 tbsp icing sugar
250ml/8fl oz/1 cup whipping cream
mint leaves to decorate
For the shortcakes
250g/8oz/2 cups plain flour
75g/3oz/1/3 cup caster sugar
15ml/1 tbsp baking powder
pinch of salt
225ml/8fl oz/1 cup whipping cream

Cook's Tip To achieve the best results when whipping cream, chill the bowl and beaters until thoroughly cold. If using an electric mixer, increase the speed gradually, and turn the bowl while beating to incorporate as much air as possible.

1 Preheat the oven to 200°C/400°F/Gas 6. Lightly grease a baking sheet.

2 To make the shortcakes, sift the flour into a mixing bowl. Add 50g/2oz/1/4 cup of the caster sugar, the baking powder and salt. Stir well.

3 Gradually add the cream, tossing lightly with a fork until the mixture forms clumps.

4 Gather the clumps together, but do not knead the dough. Shape the dough into a 15cm/6in log. Cut into six slices and place them on the prepared baking sheet.

5 Sprinkle with the remaining caster sugar. Bake for about 15 minutes until light golden brown. Leave to cool on a wire rack.

6 Meanwhile, mash a quarter of the strawberries with the icing sugar. Stir in the remaining strawberries. Leave to stand for 1 hour at room temperature.

7 Just before serving, whip the cream until soft peaks form.

8 Slice each shortcake in half. Put the bottom halves on individual plates and top with some of the cream. Divide the strawberries among the six. Replace the tops and decorate with mint. Serve with the remaining cream.

Orange Shortbread Fingers

These are a real tea-time treat. The fingers will keep in an airtight container for up to 2 weeks.

Makes 18

INGREDIENTS

115g/4oz/½ cup unsalted butter
50g/2oz/4 tbsp caster sugar, plus extra for sprinkling
finely grated rind of 2 oranges
175g/6oz/1½ cups plain flour

1 Preheat the oven to 190°C/375°F/Gas 5. Grease a large baking sheet. Beat together the butter and sugar until soft and creamy. Beat in the orange rind.

2 Gradually add the flour and gently pull the dough together to form a soft ball. Roll out the dough on a lightly floured surface to about 1cm/½in thick. Cut into fingers, sprinkle over a little extra caster sugar and put on the baking sheet. Prick the fingers with a fork and bake for about 20 minutes, until the fingers are a light golden colour.

Raspberry Sandwich Cookies

Children will love these sweet, sticky treats.

Makes 32

INGREDIENTS

115g/4oz/1 cup blanched almonds
175g/6oz/1½ cups plain flour
175g/6oz/¾ cup butter
115g/4oz/½ cup caster sugar
grated rind of 1 lemon
5ml/1 tsp vanilla essence
1 egg white
pinch of salt
40g/1½oz/⅓ cup slivered almonds, chopped
350g/12oz/1 cup raspberry jam
15ml/1 tbsp lemon juice

1 Finely grind the almonds and 45ml/3 tbsp of the flour.

2 Cream together the butter and sugar until light and fluffy. Stir in the lemon rind and vanilla essence. Add the ground almonds and remaining flour and mix well to form a dough. Gather into a ball, wrap in greaseproof paper, and chill for 1 hour. Preheat the oven to 160°C/325°F/Gas 3. Line two baking sheets with greaseproof paper.

3 Divide the dough into four. Roll each piece out on a lightly floured surface to a thickness of 3mm/⅛in. With a floured 6cm/2½in pastry cutter, stamp out circles, then stamp out the centres from half the circles.

4 When all the dough has been used, check you have equal numbers of rings and circles, then place the dough rings and circles 1cm/½in apart on the prepared baking sheets.

5 Whisk the egg white with the salt until just frothy. Brush only the cookie rings with the egg white, then sprinkle over the chopped almonds. Bake for 12–15 minutes until very lightly browned. Leave to cool for a few minutes on the sheets before transferring to a wire rack.

6 In a saucepan, melt the jam with the lemon juice until it comes to a simmer. Brush the jam over the cookie circles and sandwich together with the rings. Store in an airtight container with sheets of greaseproof paper between the layers.

Pecan Tassies

These sweet tarts accompany coffee perfectly.

Makes 24

INGREDIENTS

115g/4oz/½ cup cream cheese
115g/4oz/½ cup butter
115g/4oz/1 cup plain flour
For the filling
2 eggs
115g/4oz/⅔ cup dark brown sugar
5ml/1 tsp vanilla essence
pinch of salt
25g/1oz/2 tbsp butter, melted
115g/4oz/1 cup pecans

1 Place a baking sheet in the oven and preheat to 180°C/350°F/Gas 4. Grease 24 mini-muffin tins.

2 Chop the cream cheese and butter. Put in a mixing bowl. Sift over the flour and mix to form a dough.

3 Roll out the dough thinly. With a floured fluted pastry cutter, stamp out 24 7cm/2½in rounds. Line the muffin tins with the rounds and chill.

4 To make the filling, lightly whisk the eggs in a bowl. Gradually whisk in the brown sugar, a few tablespoons at a time, and add the vanilla essence, salt and butter. Set aside until required.

5 Reserve 24 undamaged pecan halves and chop the rest coarsely with a sharp knife.

6 Place a spoonful of chopped nuts in each muffin tin and cover with the filling. Set a pecan half on the top of each.

7 Bake on the hot baking sheet for about 20 minutes, until puffed and set. Transfer to a wire rack to cool. Serve at room temperature.

Variation To make Jam Tassies, fill the cream cheese pastry shells with raspberry or blackberry jam, or other fruit jams. Bake as described.

Pecan Puffs

Makes 24

INGREDIENTS

115g/4oz/½ cup unsalted butter
30ml/2 tbsp granulated sugar
pinch of salt
5ml/1 tsp vanilla essence
115g/4oz/1 cup pecans
115g/4oz/1 cup plain flour, sifted
icing sugar for dusting

1 Preheat the oven to 150°C/300°F/ Gas 2. Grease two baking sheets.

2 Cream the butter and sugar until light and fluffy. Stir in the salt and vanilla essence.

3 Grind the nuts in a food processor, blender or nut grinder. Stir several times to prevent nuts becoming oily.

4 Push the ground nuts through a sieve set over a bowl to aerate them. Pieces too large to go through the sieve can be ground again.

5 Stir the nuts and flour into the butter mixture to make a dough. Roll the dough into marble-size balls between the palms of your hands. Place on the prepared baking sheets and bake for 45 minutes.

6 While the puffs are still hot, roll them in icing sugar. Leave to cool completely, then roll once more in icing sugar.

Sablés with Goat's Cheese and Strawberries

Sablés are little French biscuits, made from egg yolk and butter. Crisp and slightly sweet, they contrast perfectly with the tangy goat's cheese and juicy strawberries.

Makes 24

INGREDIENTS

75g/3oz/⅓ cup butter
150g/5oz/1¼ cup plain flour
75g/3oz/¾ cup blanched hazelnuts, lightly toasted and ground
30ml/2 tbsp caster sugar
2 egg yolks beaten with 30–45ml/2–3 tbsp water
115g/4oz goat's cheese
4–6 large strawberries, cut into small pieces
hazelnuts and mint, to decorate

1 Put the butter, flour, ground hazelnuts, sugar and beaten egg yolks into a food processor and process to a smooth dough. Scrape out the dough. Shape into a log about 4cm/1½in thick. Wrap and chill.

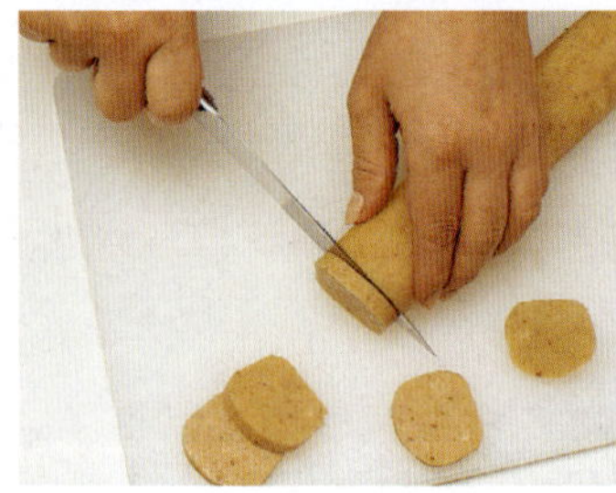

2 Preheat the oven to 200°C/400°F/Gas 6. Line a large baking sheet with non-stick baking paper. With a sharp knife, slice the dough into 5mm/¼in thick rounds and arrange on the prepared baking sheet. Bake for 7–10 minutes, until golden brown. Transfer to a wire rack to cool and crisp slightly.

3 On a plate, crumble the goat's cheese into small pieces. Mound a little goat's cheese on to each sablé, top with a piece of strawberry and sprinkle with a few hazelnuts. Serve warm.

Variation These sablés are ideal served with fruit. Beat 75g/3oz/⅓ cup cream cheese with 15ml/1 tbsp icing sugar and a little lemon or orange rind. Spread a little on the sablés and top with a few pieces of sliced kiwi fruit, peach, nectarine and a few raspberries.

Coffee Sponge Drops

These are delicious on their own, but taste even better with a filling of low-fat soft cheese and chopped stem ginger.

Makes 12

INGREDIENTS

50g/2oz/½ cup plain flour
15ml/1 tbsp instant coffee powder
2 eggs
75g/3oz/⅓ cup caster sugar
For the filling
115g/4oz/½ cup low-fat soft cheese
40g/1½oz/¼ cup chopped stem ginger

1 Preheat the oven to 190°C/375°F/Gas 5. Sift the flour and instant coffee powder together. To make the filling, beat together the soft cheese and stem ginger. Chill until required.

2 Combine the eggs and caster sugar. Beat with an electric whisk until thick and mousse-like.

3 Carefully add the sieved flour and coffee to the egg mixture and gently fold in with a metal spoon, being careful not to knock out any air.

4 Spoon the mixture into a piping bag fitted with a 1cm/½in plain nozzle. Pipe 4cm/1½in rounds on to lined baking sheets. Bake for 12 minutes. Cool on a wire rack. Sandwich together with the filling.

Lady Fingers

Named after the pale, slim fingers of highborn gentlewomen.

Makes 18

INGREDIENTS

90g/3½oz/⅔ cup plain flour
pinch of salt
4 eggs, separated
115g/4oz/½ cup granulated sugar
2.5ml/½ tsp vanilla essence
icing sugar for sprinkling

1 Preheat the oven to 150°C/300°F/Gas 2. Grease two baking sheets, then coat lightly with flour, and shake off the excess.

2 Sift the flour and salt together twice.

3 With an electric mixer, beat the egg yolks with half of the sugar until thick enough to leave a ribbon trail when the beaters are lifted.

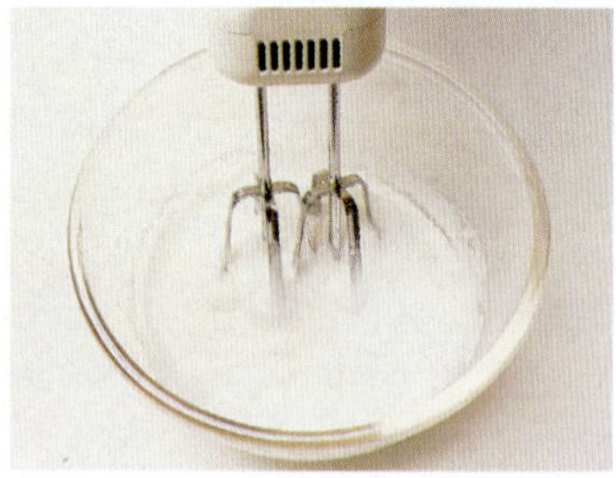

4 In another bowl, beat the egg whites until stiff. Beat in the remaining sugar until glossy.

5 Sift the flour over the yolks and spoon a large dollop of egg whites over the flour. Carefully fold in with a large metal spoon, adding the vanilla essence. Gently fold in the remaining whites.

6 Spoon the mixture into a piping bag fitted with a large plain nozzle. Pipe 10cm/4in long lines on the prepared baking sheets about 2.5cm/1in apart. Sift over a layer of icing sugar. Turn the sheet upside down to dislodge any excess sugar.

7 Bake for about 20 minutes until crusty on the outside but soft in the centre. Cool slightly on the baking sheets before transferring to a wire rack.

Walnut Cookies

Makes 60

INGREDIENTS

115g/4oz/½ cup butter or margarine
175g/6oz/¾ cup caster sugar
115g/4oz/1 cup plain flour
10ml/2 tsp vanilla essence
115g/4oz/1 cup walnuts, finely chopped

1 Preheat the oven to 150°C/300°F/Gas 2. Grease two baking sheets.

2 With an electric mixer, cream the butter or margarine until soft. Add 50g/2oz/¼ cup of the sugar and continue beating until light and fluffy. Stir in the flour, vanilla essence and walnuts. Drop teaspoonfuls of the batter 2.5–5cm/1–2in apart on the prepared baking sheets and flatten slightly. Bake for about 25 minutes.

3 Transfer to a wire rack set over a baking sheet and sprinkle with the remaining sugar.

Variation To make Almond Cookies, use an equal amount of finely chopped unblanched almonds instead of walnuts. Replace half the vanilla with 2.5ml/½ tsp almond essence.

Mocha Viennese Swirls

Makes 20

INGREDIENTS

250g/9oz plain chocolate, chopped
200g/7oz/scant 1 cup unsalted butter
50g/2oz/$^{1}/_{2}$ cup icing sugar
30ml/2 tbsp strong black coffee
200g/7oz/1$^{3}/_{4}$ cups plain flour
50g/2oz/$^{1}/_{2}$ cup cornflour
about 20 blanched almonds

Cook's Tip If the mixture is too stiff to pipe, soften it with a little more black coffee.

1 Preheat the oven to 190°C/375°F/Gas 5. Lightly grease two large baking sheets. Melt 115g/4oz of the chocolate in a heatproof bowl over a saucepan of hot water. Cream the butter with the icing sugar in a bowl until smooth and pale. Beat in the melted chocolate, then the strong black coffee.

2 Sift the flour and cornflour over the mixture. Fold in lightly and evenly to make a soft mixture.

3 Spoon the mixture into a piping bag fitted with a large star nozzle and pipe 20 swirls on the prepared baking sheets, allowing room for spreading during baking.

4 Press an almond into the centre of each swirl. Bake for about 15 minutes, until the biscuits are firm and just beginning to brown. Leave to cool for about 10 minutes on the baking sheets, then lift carefully on to a wire rack to cool completely.

5 Melt the remaining chocolate and dip the base of each swirl to coat. Place on a sheet of non-stick baking paper and leave to set.

Chocolate Amaretti

Makes 24

INGREDIENTS

150g/5oz/1¼ cups blanched whole almonds
90g/3½oz/scant ½ cup caster sugar
15ml/1 tbsp cocoa powder
30ml/2 tbsp icing sugar
2 egg whites
pinch of cream of tartar
5ml/1 tsp almond essence
flaked almonds, to decorate

1 Preheat the oven to 180°C/350°F/Gas 4. Place the almonds on a baking sheet and bake for 10–12 minutes until golden brown. Leave to cool. Reduce the oven temperature to 160°C/325°F/Gas 3. Line a large baking sheet with non-stick baking paper. In a food processor, process the almonds with half the sugar until they are finely ground but not oily. Transfer to a bowl and sift in the cocoa and icing sugar. Set aside.

2 In a mixing bowl with an electric mixer, beat the egg whites and cream of tartar until stiff peaks form. Sprinkle in the remaining sugar a tablespoon at a time, beating well after each addition, and continue beating until the whites are glossy and stiff. Beat in the almond essence.

3 Sprinkle over the almond-sugar mixture and gently fold into the beaten egg whites until just blended. Spoon the mixture into a large piping bag fitted with a plain 1cm/½in nozzle. Pipe 4cm/1½in rounds about 2.5cm/1in apart on the prepared baking sheet. Press a flaked almond into the centre of each.

4 Bake the cookies for 12–15 minutes, or until crisp. Remove the baking sheets to a wire rack to cool for 10 minutes. With a metal palette knife, remove the amarettis to a wire rack to cool completely.

Decorated Chocolate Lebkuchen

Wrapped in paper or cellophane, or beautifully boxed, these decorated cookies make a lovely present. Don't make them too far in advance as the chocolate will gradually discolour.

Makes 40

INGREDIENTS

1 quantity Lebkuchen mixture
115g/4oz plain chocolate, chopped
115g/4oz milk chocolate, chopped
115g/4oz white chocolate, chopped
chocolate vermicelli, for sprinkling
cocoa powder or icing sugar for dusting

1 Grease two baking sheets. Roll out just over half of the Lebkuchen mixture until 5mm/¼in thick. Cut out heart shapes, using a 4.5cm/1¾in heart-shaped cutter. Transfer to baking sheet. Gather the trimmings together with the remaining dough and cut into 20 pieces. Roll into balls and place on the baking sheet. Flatten each ball slightly with your fingers.

2 Chill both sheets for 30 minutes. Preheat the oven to 180°C/350°F/Gas 4. Bake for 8–10 minutes. Cool on a wire rack.

3 Melt the plain chocolate in a heatproof bowl over a small saucepan of hot water. Melt the milk and white chocolate in separate bowls.

4 Make three small paper piping bags out of greaseproof paper. Spoon a little of each chocolate into the three paper piping bags and reserve. Spoon a little plain chocolate over one third of the biscuits, spreading it slightly to cover them completely. (Tapping the rack gently will help the chocolate to run down the sides.)

5 Snip the merest tip from the bag of white chocolate and drizzle it over some of the coated biscuits, to give a decorative finish.

6 Sprinkle the chocolate vermicelli over the plain chocolate-coated biscuits that haven't been decorated. Coat the remaining biscuits with the milk and white chocolate and decorate some of these with more chocolate from the piping bags, contrasting the colours. Scatter more undecorated biscuits with vermicelli. Leave the biscuits to set.

7 Transfer the undecorated biscuits to a plate or tray and dust lightly with cocoa powder or icing sugar.

Cook's Tip If the chocolate in the bowls starts to set before you have finished decorating, put the bowls back over the heat for 1–2 minutes. If the chocolate in the piping bags starts to harden, microwave briefly or put in a clean bowl over a pan of simmering water until soft.

Chocolate Fruit and Nut Cookies

These simple, chunky gingerbread biscuits make a delicious gift, especially when presented in a decorative gift box. The combination of walnuts, almonds and cherries is very effective, but you can use any other mixture of glacé fruits and nuts.

Makes 20

INGREDIENTS

50g/2oz/4 tbsp caster sugar
75ml/3fl oz/1/3 cup water
225g/8oz plain chocolate, chopped
40g/1 1/2oz/3/4 cup walnut halves
75g/3oz/1/3 cup glacé cherries, chopped into small wedges
115g/4oz/1 cup whole blanched almonds
For the Lebkuchen
115g/4oz/1/2 cup unsalted butter
115g/4oz/2/3 cup light muscovado sugar
1 egg, beaten
115g/4oz/1/3 cup black treacle
400g/14oz/3 1/2 cups self-raising flour
5ml/1 tsp ground ginger
2.5ml/1/2 tsp ground cloves
1.5ml/1/4 tsp chilli powder

Cook's Tip Carefully stack the biscuits in a pretty box or tin, lined with tissue paper, or tie in cellophane bundles.

1 To make the Lebkuchen, cream together the butter and sugar until pale and fluffy. Beat in the egg and black treacle. Sift the flour, ginger, cloves and chilli powder into the bowl. Using a wooden spoon, gradually mix the ingredients together to make a stiff paste. Turn on to a lightly floured work surface and knead lightly until smooth. Wrap and chill for 30 minutes.

2 Preheat the oven to 180°C/350°F/Gas 4. Grease two baking sheets. Shape the dough into a roll, 20cm/8in long. Chill for 30 minutes. Cut into 20 slices and space them on the baking sheets. Bake for 10 minutes. Leave on the baking sheets for 5 minutes and then transfer to a wire rack and leave to cool.

3 Put the sugar and water in a small, heavy-based saucepan. Heat gently until the sugar dissolves. Bring to the boil and boil for 1 minute, until slightly syrupy. Leave for 3 minutes, to cool slightly, and then stir in the chocolate until it has melted and made a smooth sauce.

4 Place the wire rack of biscuits over a large tray or board. Spoon a little of the chocolate mixture over the biscuits, spreading it to the edges with the back of the spoon.

5 Gently press a walnut half into the centre of each biscuit. Arrange pieces of glacé cherry and almonds alternately around the nuts. Leave to set in a cool place.

Chocolate Almond Torronne

Serve this Italian speciality in thin slices.

Makes 20

INGREDIENTS

115g/4oz plain chocolate, chopped
50g/2oz/4 tbsp unsalted butter
1 egg white
115g/4oz/½ cup caster sugar
50g/2oz/½ cup ground almonds
75g/3oz/¾ cup chopped toasted almonds
75ml/5 tbsp chopped candied peel
For the coating
175g/6oz white chocolate, chopped
25g/1oz/2 tbsp unsalted butter
115g/4oz/1 cup flaked almonds, toasted

1 Melt the chocolate with the butter in a heatproof bowl over a saucepan of hot water, stirring until the mixture is smooth.

2 In a clean, grease-free bowl, whisk the egg white with the sugar until stiff. Gradually beat in the melted chocolate, then stir in the ground almonds, chopped toasted almonds and peel.

3 Tip the mixture on to a large sheet of non-stick baking paper and shape into a thick roll.

4 As the mixture cools, use the paper to press the roll firmly into a triangular shape. Twist the paper over the triangular roll and chill until completely set.

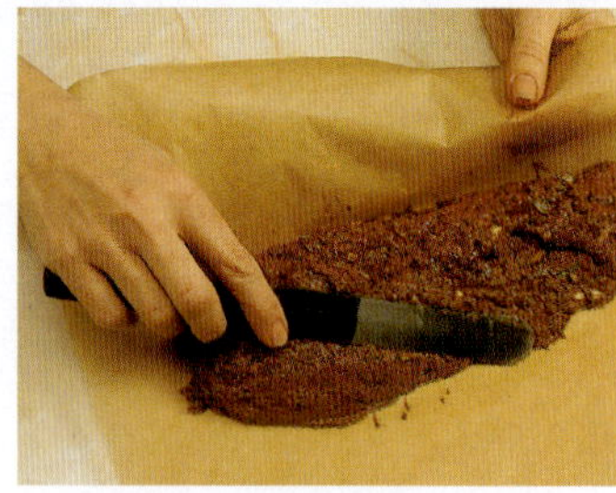

5 To make the coating, melt the white chocolate with the butter in a heatproof bowl over a saucepan of hot water. Unwrap the chocolate roll and spread the white chocolate quickly over the surface. Press the almonds in a thin even coating over the chocolate, working quickly before the chocolate sets.

6 Chill again until firm, then cut the torronne into fairly thin slices to serve.

Cook's Tip The mixture can be shaped into a simple round roll instead of the triangular shape if you prefer.

Chocolate Hazelnut Galettes

There's stacks of sophistication in these triple-tiered chocolate rounds sandwiched with a light fromage frais filling.

Makes 4

INGREDIENTS

175g/6oz plain chocolate, chopped
45ml/3 tbsp single cream
30ml/2 tbsp flaked hazelnuts
115g/4oz white chocolate, chopped
175g/6oz/¾ cup fromage frais
15ml/1 tbsp dry sherry
60ml/4 tbsp finely chopped hazelnuts, toasted
physalis (Cape gooseberries), dipped in white chocolate, to decorate

1 Melt the plain chocolate in a heatproof bowl over a saucepan of hot water, then remove from the heat and stir in the cream.

2 Draw 12 7.5cm/3in circles on sheets of non-stick baking paper. Turn the paper over and spread the plain chocolate over each marked circle, covering in a thin, even layer. Scatter flaked hazelnuts over four of the circles, then leave until set.

3 Melt the white chocolate in a heatproof bowl over a saucepan of hot water, then stir in the fromage frais and dry sherry. Fold in the chopped, toasted hazelnuts. Leave to cool until the mixture holds its shape.

Cook's Tip The chocolate could be spread over heart shapes instead, for a special Valentine's Day dessert.

4 Remove the plain chocolate rounds carefully from the paper and sandwich them together in stacks of 3, spooning the white chocolate hazelnut cream between each layer and using the hazelnut-covered rounds on top. Chill before serving.

5 To serve, place the galettes on individual plates and decorate with chocolate-dipped physalis.

Savoury Treats

The earliest cookies were savoury, made with just flour, water and perhaps some salt, but as the practice of cookie-making became established the savoury version lost ground to sweet cookies. Now, there is a trend towards more savoury tastes with more wine being drunk, and quaffed more casually rather than consumed only as an accompaniment to special meals, and savoury cookies are making a comeback. This time, though, the recipes are far more varied and appetising. Variety is introduced by using different flours, and including ingredients such as oats, polenta and nuts for texture. Savoury cookie doughs are flavoured with cheese, herbs and spices, or topped with sesame or other seeds for extra crunch and savour.

Try sandwiching savoury cookies together in pairs with soft cheese, simply seasoned or flavoured with a complementary ingredient, such as chives with cheese biscuits. Triple-deckers can be created in the same way. Avoid filling cookies too far in advance, though, in case they soften.

Any type of savoury cookie is versatile – it can be served with drinks, soups and cheese, or taken in packed lunches and picnics.

Festive Nibbles

Shape these spicy cheese snacks in any way you wish – stars, crescent moons, triangles, squares, hearts, fingers or rounds. Serve them with drinks from ice-cold cocktails to hot and spicy mulls.

Makes 60

INGREDIENTS

115g/4oz/1 cup plain flour, plus extra for dusting
5ml/1 tsp mustard powder
pinch of salt
115g/4oz/½ cup butter
75g/3oz/¾ cup Cheddar cheese, grated
pinch of cayenne pepper
30ml/2 tbsp water
1 egg, beaten
poppy seeds, sunflower seeds or sesame seeds, to decorate

1 Preheat the oven to 200°C/400°F/Gas 6. Grease two baking sheets. Sift the flour, mustard powder and salt into a bowl and rub in the butter until the mixture resembles fine breadcrumbs.

2 Stir in the cheese and cayenne pepper and sprinkle on the water. Add half the beaten egg, mix to a firm dough and knead lightly until smooth.

3 Roll out the dough on a lightly floured surface and cut out a variety of shapes. Re-roll the trimmings and cut more shapes.

4 Place on the prepared baking sheets and brush with the remaining egg. Sprinkle on the seeds. Bake for 8–10 minutes until golden.

Cheese Straws

Makes 50 straws and 8 rings

INGREDIENTS

115g/4oz/1 cup plain flour, plus extra for dusting
5ml/1 tsp mustard powder
pinch of salt
115g/4oz/½ cup butter
75g/3oz/¾ cup Cheddar cheese, grated
pinch of cayenne pepper
30ml/2 tbsp water
1 egg, beaten
poppy seeds, sunflower seeds or sesame seeds, to decorate

1 Make the cheese pastry in the same way as Festive Nibbles. Cut the cheese pastry into fingers about 10cm/4in long and 5mm/¼in wide.

2 Roll out the trimmings, cut rounds using two pastry cutters of different sizes, a 6cm/2½in one to cut out the circle and a 5cm/2in diameter one to stamp out the centre. Cook as above.

3 To serve, push six or eight straws through each ring.

Savoury Cheese Whirls

This make a tasty tea-time treat for children.

Makes 16

INGREDIENTS

250g/9oz frozen puff pastry, defrosted
2.5ml/½ tsp vegetable extract
1 egg, beaten
50g/2oz/½ cup grated red Leicester, or Cheddar cheese
carrot and cucumber sticks, to serve

1 Preheat the oven to 220°C/425°F/ Gas 7. Grease a large baking sheet. Roll out the pastry on a floured surface to a large rectangle, about 35 x 25cm/14 x 10in.

2 Spread the pastry with vegetable extract, leaving a 1cm/½in border. Brush the edges of the pastry with egg and sprinkle over the cheese to cover the vegetable extract.

3 Roll the pastry up quite tightly like a Swiss roll, starting from a longer edge. Brush the outside of the pastry with beaten egg.

4 Cut the pastry roll into thick slices and place on the prepared baking sheet.

5 Bake for 12–15 minutes, until the pastry is well risen and golden. Arrange on a serving plate and serve warm or cold with carrot and cucumber sticks.

Cook's Tip If the shapes become a little squashed when sliced, re-form into rounds by opening out the layers with the end of a knife.

Variation Omit the vegetable extract and use peanut butter, if preferred.

Cream Cheese Spirals

Makes 32

INGREDIENTS

225g/8oz/1 cup butter
225g/8oz/1 cup cream cheese
10ml/2 tsp granulated sugar
225g/8oz/2 cups plain flour
1 egg white beaten with 15ml/ 1 tbsp water, for glazing
granulated sugar for sprinkling
For the filling
115g/4oz/1 cup walnuts or pecans, finely chopped
75g/3oz/½ cup light brown sugar
5ml/1 tsp ground cinnamon

1 With an electric mixer, cream the butter, cream cheese, and sugar until soft. Sift over the flour and mix to form a dough. Gather into a ball and divide into halves. Flatten each piece, wrap in greaseproof paper and chill for at least 30 minutes.

2 To make the filling, mix together the chopped walnuts or pecans, brown sugar and cinnamon.

3 Preheat the oven to 190°C/375°F/ Gas 5. Grease two baking sheets.

4 Roll out each half of dough thinly into a circle about 28cm/11in in diameter. Trim the edges with a knife, using a dinner plate as a guide.

5 Brush the surface with the egg white glaze and sprinkle the dough evenly with half the filling.

6 Cut the dough into quarters and each quarter into four sections, to form 16 triangles.

7 Starting from the base of the triangles, roll up to form spirals.

8 Place on the prepared baking sheets and brush with the remaining glaze. Sprinkle with granulated sugar. Bake for 15–20 minutes until golden. Transfer to a wire rack.

Bacon Twists

Making bread is always fun, so try this savoury version and add that extra twist to breakfast. Serve with soft cheese with herbs.

Makes 12

INGREDIENTS

450g/1lb/4 cups strong white flour
1 sachet easy-blend yeast
pinch of salt
400ml/14fl oz/1²/₃ cups hand-hot water
12 streaky bacon rashers
1 egg, beaten

Cook's Tip The same basic dough mix can be used to make rolls or a loaf of bread. Tap the base of the loaf – if it sounds hollow, it's cooked.

1 Mix the flour, yeast and salt in a bowl and stir them together. Add a little of the water and mix with a knife. Add the remaining water and use your hands to pull the mixture together, to make a sticky dough.

2 Turn the dough on to a lightly floured surface and knead for 5 minutes, until the dough is smooth and stretchy.

3 Divide the dough into 12 even-size pieces and roll each one into a sausage shape. Lightly oil a baking sheet.

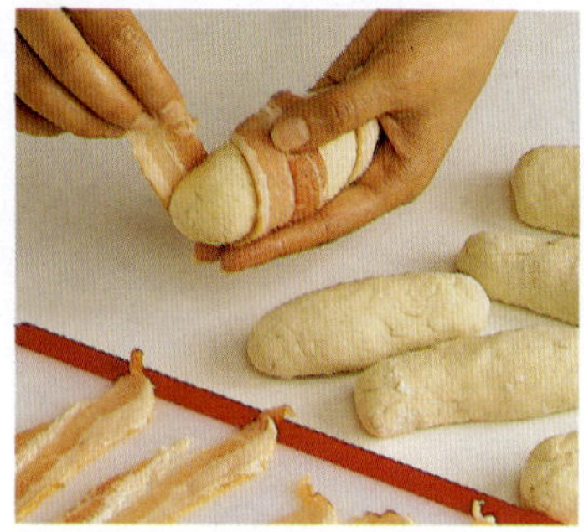

4 Place each bacon rasher on a chopping board and run the back of the knife down its length, to stretch it slightly. Wind a rasher of bacon round each dough 'sausage'.

5 Brush the 'sausages' with beaten egg and arrange them on the prepared baking sheet. Leave in a warm place for 30 minutes, until doubled in size. Preheat the oven to 200°C/400°F/Gas 6. Bake the 'sausages' for 20–25 minutes, until cooked and browned.

Variations Make some meat-free versions of these twists for vegetarians by twisting the dough by hand and sprinkling with poppy or sesame seeds before baking.

Wisconsin Cheddar and Chive Biscuits

These soft biscuits are delicious warm, split and spread with butter; serve with soup or as part of a main dish.

Makes 20

INGREDIENTS

200g/7oz/1¾ cups plain flour
10ml/2 tsp baking powder
2.5ml/½ tsp bicarbonate of soda
pinch of salt
1.5ml/¼ tsp black pepper
65g/2½oz/5 tbsp unsalted butter, chopped
50g/2oz/½ cup grated mature Cheddar cheese
30ml/2 tbsp chopped fresh chives
175ml/6fl oz/¾ cup buttermilk

Variation For Cheddar and Bacon Biscuits, substitute 45ml/3 tbsp crumbled cooked bacon for the chives.

1 Preheat the oven to 200°C/400°F/Gas 6. Grease a baking sheet.

2 Sift the flour, baking powder, bicarbonate of soda, salt and pepper into a large bowl. Rub the butter into the dry ingredients until the mixture resembles coarse breadcrumbs. Add the cheese and chives and stir to mix.

3 Make a well in the centre of the mixture. Add the buttermilk and stir vigorously until the batter comes away from the sides of the bowl.

4 Drop in 30ml/2 tbsp mounds spaced 5–7.5cm/2–3in apart on the prepared baking sheet. Bake for 12–15 minutes, until golden brown.

Corn Oysters

Serve hot by themselves or as an accompaniment to meat or chicken dishes.

Makes about 8

INGREDIENTS

150g/5oz/1 cup grated fresh sweetcorn kernels
1 egg, separated
30ml/2 tbsp plain flour
pinch of salt
1.5ml/¼ tsp black pepper
25–50g/1–2oz/2–4 tbsp butter or margarine
30–50ml/1–2fl oz/2–4 tbsp vegetable oil

1 Combine the corn, egg yolk and flour in a bowl. Mix well. Add the salt and pepper.

2 In a separate bowl, beat the egg white until it forms stiff peaks. Fold it carefully into the corn mixture.

3 Heat 30ml/2 tbsp butter or margarine with 30ml/2 tbsp oil in a frying pan. When the fats are very hot and almost smoking, drop tablespoonfuls of the corn mixture into the pan. Fry until crisp and brown on the undersides.

4 Turn the 'oysters' over and cook for 1–2 minutes on the other side. Drain on paper towels and keep hot. Continue frying the 'oysters', adding more fat as necessary.

Cook's Tip Thawed frozen or canned sweetcorn kernels can also be used. Drain them well and chop.

Cornmeal Biscuits

Serve these cookies hot, spread with butter.

Makes 12

INGREDIENTS

175g/6oz/1¼ cups plain flour
12.5ml/2½ tsp baking powder
pinch of salt
50g/2oz/½ cup cornmeal, plus extra for sprinkling
175g/6oz/⅓ cup lard or butter, chopped
175ml/6fl oz/¾ cup milk

1 Preheat the oven to 230°C/450°F/Gas 8. Sprinkle an ungreased baking sheet lightly with cornmeal.

2 Sift the flour, baking powder and salt into a bowl. Stir in the cornmeal. Rub the lard or butter into the dry ingredients until the mixture resembles coarse breadcrumbs.

3 Make a well in the centre and pour in the milk. Stir in quickly with a wooden spoon until the dough begins to pull away from the sides.

4 Turn the dough on to a lightly floured surface and knead lightly 8–10 times only. Roll out to a thickness of 1cm/½in. Cut into rounds with a floured 5cm/2in biscuit cutter.

5 Arrange on the prepared baking sheet, about 2.5cm/1in apart. Sprinkle with cornmeal. Bake for 10–12 minutes, until golden brown.

Thyme and Mustard Biscuits

These aromatic biscuits are delicious served with herby cheese as a light savoury last course.

Makes 40

INGREDIENTS

175g/6oz/1½ cups wholemeal plain flour
50g/2oz/⅔ cup medium oatmeal
25g/1oz/2 tbsp caster sugar
10ml/2 tsp baking powder
30ml/2 tbsp fresh thyme leaves
50g/2oz/4 tbsp butter, chopped
25g/1oz/2 tbsp white vegetable fat, chopped
45ml/3 tbsp milk
10ml/2 tsp Dijon mustard
30ml/2 tbsp sesame seeds
salt and black pepper

1 Preheat the oven to 200°C/400°F/Gas 6. Grease two baking sheets. Put the flour, oatmeal, sugar, baking powder, thyme leaves and seasoning into a bowl and mix. Add the fats to the bowl, then rub in.

2 Mix the milk and mustard together and stir into the flour mixture until you have a soft dough.

3 Knead lightly on a floured surface then roll out to a thickness of 5mm/¼in. Stamp out 5cm/2in rounds with a floured fluted biscuit cutter and arrange, spaced slightly apart, on the prepared baking sheets.

4 Re-roll the trimmings and continue stamping out biscuits until all the dough is used. Prick the biscuits with a fork and sprinkle with sesame seeds. Cook for 10–12 minutes, until lightly browned.

5 Cool on the sheets then pack into a small airtight container. Store in a cool place for up to 5 days.

Salted Peanut Cookies

The combinaton of salt and sweet flavours is delicious.

Makes 70

INGREDIENTS

350g/12oz/3 cups plain flour
2.5ml/½ tsp bicarbonate of soda
115g/4oz/½ cup butter
115g/4oz/½ cup margarine
250g/9oz/1½ cups light brown sugar
2 eggs
10ml/2 tsp vanilla essence
225g/8oz/2 cups salted peanuts

1 Preheat the oven to 190°C/375°F/ Gas 5. Lightly grease two baking sheets. Grease the bottom of a glass and dip in sugar.

2 Sift together the flour and bicarbonate of soda. Set aside.

3 With an electric mixer, cream the butter, margarine and sugar until light and fluffy. Beat in the eggs and vanilla essence. Fold in the flour mixture.

Variation To make Cashew Cookies, substitute an equal amount of salted cashews for the peanuts, and add as above. The flavour is subtle and interesting.

4 Stir the peanuts into the butter mixture until evenly combined.

5 Drop teaspoonfuls 5cm/2in apart on the prepared sheets. Flatten with the prepared glass.

6 Bake for about 10 minutes, until lightly coloured. With a metal spatula, transfer to a wire rack to cool completely.

Cheddar Pennies

Serve these tasty snacks with pre-dinner drinks.

Makes 20

INGREDIENTS

50g/2oz/4 tbsp butter
115g/4oz/1 cup Cheddar cheese, grated
40g/1½oz/⅓ cup plain flour
pinch of salt
pinch of chilli powder

1 With an electric mixer, cream the butter until soft.

2 Stir in the cheese, flour, salt and chilli. Gather to form a dough.

3 Transfer to a lightly floured surface. Shape into a cylinder about 3cm/1¼in in diameter. Wrap in greaseproof paper and chill for 1–2 hours.

4 Preheat the oven to 180°C/350°F/ Gas 4. Grease 1–2 baking sheets.

5 Cut the dough into 5mm/¼in thick slices and place on the prepared baking sheets. Bake for about 15 minutes, until golden. Transfer to a wire rack to cool.

Blue Cheese and Chive Crisps

Makes 48

INGREDIENTS

225g/8oz/2 cups blue cheese, crumbled
115g/4oz/½ cup unsalted butter
1 egg
1 egg yolk
30ml/2 tsp chopped fresh chives
black pepper
225g/8oz/2 cups plain flour, sifted

Cook's Tip The cheese crisps will keep up to 10 days in an airtight container.

1 The day before serving, beat together the cheese and butter until well blended. Add the egg, egg yolk, chives and a little pepper and beat until just blended.

2 Add the flour in three batches, folding in well between each addition.

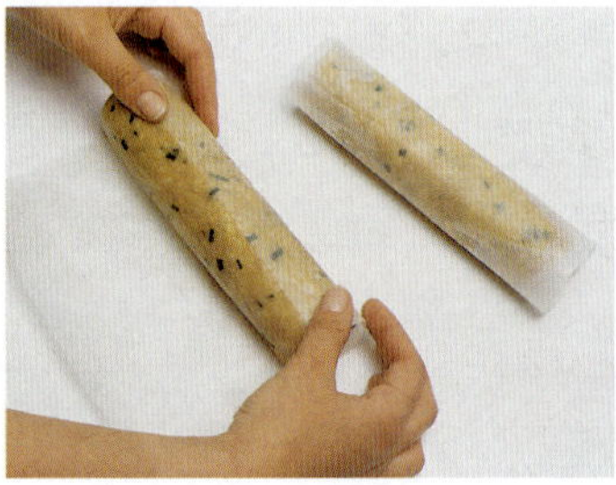

3 Divide the dough in half and shape each half into a log about 5cm/2in in diameter. Wrap in greaseproof paper and chill overnight. Preheat the oven to 190°C/375°F/Gas 5. Lightly grease two baking sheets.

4 Cut the dough logs across into slices about 3mm/⅛in thick. Place on the prepared baking sheets. Bake for about 10 minutes, until just golden around the edges. Transfer to a wire rack to cool.

Cheese Muffins

Makes 9

INGREDIENTS

50g/2oz/4 tbsp butter
175g/6oz/1½ cups plain flour
10ml/2 tsp baking powder
30ml/2 tbsp caster sugar
pinch of salt
5ml/1 tsp paprika
2 eggs
120ml/4fl oz/½ cup milk
5ml/1 tsp dried thyme
50g/2oz mature Cheddar cheese, cut into 1cm/½in dice

1 Preheat the oven to 190°C/375°F/ Gas 5. Grease nine muffin tins, or use paper liners. Melt the butter in a small saucepan.

2 In a mixing bowl, sift together the flour, baking powder, sugar, salt and paprika.

3 In another bowl, combine the eggs, milk, melted butter and thyme and whisk to blend.

4 Add the milk mixture to the dry ingredients and stir until just moistened; do not mix until smooth.

5 Place a heaped spoonful of batter into the prepared tins. Drop a few pieces of cheese over each, then top with another spoonful of batter.

6 Bake for about 25 minutes, until puffed and golden. Leave to stand for 5 minutes before unmoulding on to a wire rack. These muffins are best served warm or at room temperature.

Bacon Cornmeal Muffins

Serve these muffins fresh from the oven for a special breakfast.

Makes 14

INGREDIENTS

8 bacon rashers
50g/2oz/4 tbsp butter
50g/2oz/4 tbsp margarine
115g/4oz/1 cup plain flour
15ml/1 tbsp baking powder
5ml/1 tsp caster sugar
pinch of salt
175g/6oz/1½ cups cornmeal
250ml/8fl oz/1 cup milk
2 eggs

1 Preheat the oven to 200°C/400°F/ Gas 6. Grease 14 muffin tins, or use paper liners.

2 Fry the bacon until crisp. Drain on paper towels, then chop into small pieces. Set aside. Melt the butter and margarine in a saucepan over a low heat and set aside.

3 Sift the flour, baking powder, sugar and salt into a large mixing bowl. Stir in the cornmeal, then make a well in the centre. In another saucepan, heat the milk to lukewarm. In a small bowl, lightly whisk the eggs, then add to the milk. Stir in the melted fats.

4 Pour the milk mixture into the centre of the well and stir until smooth and well blended.

5 Fold in the bacon. Spoon the batter into the prepared tins, filling them halfway. Bake for about 20 minutes, until risen and lightly coloured.

Savoury Parmesan Puffs

Makes 6

INGREDIENTS

115g/4oz/½ cup freshly grated Parmesan cheese
115g/4oz/1 cup plain flour
pinch of salt
15ml/1 tbsp butter or margarine
2 eggs
250ml/8fl oz/1 cup milk

1 Preheat the oven to 230°C/450°F/Gas 8. Grease six individual baking tins. Sprinkle each tin with 15ml/1 tbsp of the grated Parmesan. Alternatively, you can use ramekins, in which case, heat them on a baking sheet in the oven then grease and sprinkle with Parmesan just before filling. Sift the flour and salt into a small bowl. Set aside. Melt the butter or margarine in a small saucepan.

2 In a mixing bowl, beat together the eggs, milk and melted butter or margarine. Add the flour mixture and stir until smoothly blended.

3 Divide the batter evenly among the containers, filling each one about half full. Bake for 15 minutes, then sprinkle the tops of the puffs with the remaining grated Parmesan cheese. Reduce the heat to 180°C/350°F/Gas 4 and continue baking for 20–25 minutes, until the puffs are firm and golden brown.

4 Remove the puffs from the oven. To unmould, run a thin knife around the inside of each container to loosen them. Gently ease out, then transfer to a wire rack to cool.

Herb Popovers

Makes 12

INGREDIENTS

25g/1oz/2 tbsp butter
3 eggs
250ml/8fl oz/1 cup milk
175g/6oz/¾ cup plain flour
pinch of salt
1 small sprig each mixed fresh herbs, such as chives, tarragon, dill and parsley

1 Preheat the oven to 220°C/425°F/ Gas 7. Grease 12 small ramekins or popover tins. Melt the butter in a small saucepan over a low heat.

2 With an electric mixer, beat the eggs until blended. Beat in the milk and melted butter.

3 Sift together the flour and salt, then beat into the egg mixture to combine thoroughly.

4 Strip the herb leaves from the stems and chop finely. Stir 30ml/ 2 tbsp into the batter.

5 Pour the batter into the prepared dishes or tins so they are half full.

6 Bake for 25–30 minutes, until golden. Do not open the oven door during baking time or the popovers may fall. For drier popovers, pierce each one with a knife after 30 minutes baking time and bake for 5 minutes more. Serve hot.

Cheese Popovers

Makes 12

INGREDIENTS

25ml/1½ tbsp butter
3 eggs
250ml/8fl oz/1 cup milk
75g/3oz/¾ cup plain flour
pinch of salt
1.5ml/¼ tsp paprika
75g/3oz/6 tbsp freshly grated Parmesan cheese

1 Preheat the oven to 220°C/425°F/ Gas 7. Grease 12 small ramekins or popover tins. Melt the butter in a small saucepan over a low heat.

2 With an electric mixer, beat the eggs until blended. Beat in the milk and melted butter.

3 Sift together the flour, salt, and paprika, then beat into the egg mixture. Add the cheese and stir.

4 Fill the prepared dishes or tins so they are half full. Bake for 25–30 minutes, until golden. Do not open the oven door during baking or the popovers will fall. For drier popovers, pierce each one with a knife after 30 minutes baking time and bake for 5 minutes more. Serve hot.

Tiny Cheese Puffs

These bite-sized portions of choux pastry are the ideal accompaniment to a glass of wine before dinner.

Makes 45

INGREDIENTS

115g/4oz/1 cup plain flour
pinch of salt
5ml/1 tsp dry mustard powder
pinch of cayenne pepper
250ml/8fl oz/1 cup water
115g/4oz/½ cup butter, chopped
4 eggs
75g/3oz Gruyère cheese, finely diced
15ml/1 tbsp finely chopped chives

Cook's Tip The puffs can be prepared ahead and are suitable for freezing. Reheat in a hot oven for 5 minutes, until crisp, before serving.

1 Preheat the oven to 200°C/400°F/Gas 6. Lightly grease two large baking sheets. Sift together the flour, salt, dry mustard and cayenne pepper.

2 In a medium-size saucepan, bring the water and butter to the boil over a medium-high heat. Remove from the heat and add the flour mixture all at once, beating with a wooden spoon until the dough forms a ball. Return to the heat and beat constantly for 1–2 minutes to dry out. Remove from the heat and cool for 3–5 minutes.

3 Beat three of the eggs in to the dough, one at a time, beating well after each addition. Beat the fourth egg in a small bowl and add a teaspoon at a time, beating until the dough is smooth and shiny and falls slowly when dropped from a spoon. (You may not need all of the fourth egg; reserve any remaining egg for glazing.) Stir in the diced cheese and chives.

4 Using two teaspoons, drop small mounds of dough 5cm/2in apart on to the prepared baking sheets. Beat the reserved egg with 15ml/1 tbsp water and brush the tops with the glaze.

5 Bake for 8 minutes, then reduce the oven temperature to 180°C/350°F/Gas 4 and bake for 7–8 minutes more, until puffed and golden. Transfer to a wire rack to cool. Serve warm.

Variation For Ham and Cheese Puffs, add 50g/2oz/¼ cup finely diced ham with the cheese. For Cheesy Herb Puffs, stir in 30ml/2 tbsp chopped fresh herbs or spring onions with the cheese.

Cheese Scones

These delicious scones make a good tea-time treat. They are best served fresh and still slightly warm.

Makes 12

INGREDIENTS

225g/8oz/2 cups plain flour
12.5ml/2½ tsp baking powder
2.5ml/½ tsp dry mustard powder
2.5ml/½ tsp salt
50g/2oz/4 tbsp cold butter, chopped
75g/3oz/¾ cup Cheddar cheese, grated
150ml/¼ pint/⅔ cup milk
1 egg, beaten

1 Preheat the oven to 230°C/450°F/ Gas 8. Sift the flour, baking powder, mustard powder and salt into a mixing bowl. Add the butter and rub into the flour mixture until the mixture resembles breadcrumbs.

2 Stir in 50g/2oz/½ cup of the cheese into the butter and flour mixture.

3 Make a well in the centre and gently stir in the milk and egg until smooth. Turn the dough on to a lightly floured surface.

4 Roll out the dough and cut into triangles or squares. Brush lightly with milk and sprinkle with the remaining cheese. Leave to rest for 15 minutes, then bake for 15 minutes, until well risen.

Oatcakes

These are very simple to make and are an excellent addition to a cheese board.

Makes 24

INGREDIENTS

225g/8oz/2 cups medium oatmeal, plus extra for sprinkling
75g/3oz/¾ cup plain flour
1.5ml/¼ tsp bicarbonate of soda
5ml/1 tsp salt
25g/1oz/2 tbsp lard
25g/1oz/2 tbsp butter

1 Preheat the oven to 220°C/425°F/ Gas 7. Place the oatmeal, flour, bicarbonate of soda and salt in a large bowl. Melt the two fats together in a small saucepan over a low heat.

2 Add the melted fat and enough boiling water to make a dough. Turn on to a surface sprinkled with a little oatmeal. Roll out thinly and cut into 24 circles. Bake on ungreased baking sheets for 15 minutes.

Ham and Tomato Scones

These make an ideal accompaniment for soup. Choose a strongly flavoured ham and chop it fairly finely, so that a little goes a long way.

Makes 12

INGREDIENTS

225g/8oz/2 cups self-raising flour
5ml/1 tsp dry mustard
5ml/1 tsp paprika, plus extra for sprinkling
pinch of salt
25g/1oz/2 tbsp margarine, chopped
15ml/1 tbsp snipped fresh basil
50g/2oz/1/3 cup drained sun-dried tomatoes in oil, chopped
50g/2oz Black Forest ham, chopped
90–120ml/3–4fl oz/1/4–1/2 cup skimmed milk, plus extra for brushing.

1 Preheat the oven to 200°C/400°F/Gas 6. Flour a large baking sheet. Sift the flour, mustard, paprika and salt into a bowl. Using your fingers, rub in the margarine until the mixture resembles breadcrumbs.

2 Stir the basil, sun-dried tomatoes and ham into the bowl. Pour in enough milk to make a soft dough.

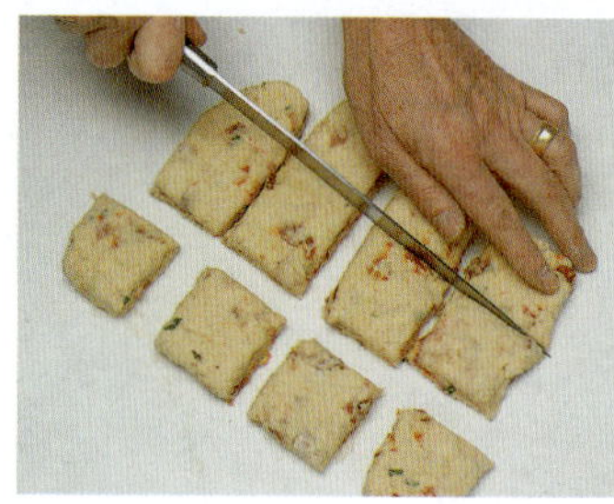

3 Turn the dough on to a lightly floured surface, knead lightly and roll out to a 20 x 15cm/8 x 6in rectangle. Cut into 5cm/2in squares and arrange on the baking sheet.

4 Brush the tops with milk, sprinkle with paprika and bake for 12–15 minutes. Transfer to a rack to cool.

Feta Cheese and Chive Scones

Feta cheese makes an excellent substitute for butter in these tangy savoury scones.

Makes 9

INGREDIENTS

115g/4oz/1 cup self-raising white flour
150g/5oz/1 cup self-raising wholemeal flour
pinch of salt
75g/3oz feta cheese
15ml/1 tbsp snipped fresh chives
150ml/¼ pint/⅔ cup skimmed milk, plus extra for glazing
1.5ml/¼ tsp cayenne pepper

1 Preheat the oven to 200°C/400°F/ Gas 6. Sift the flours and salt into a mixing bowl, adding any bran left over from the flour in the sieve.

2 Crumble the feta cheese and rub into the dry ingredients. Stir in the chives, then add the milk and mix to a soft dough.

3 Turn on to a floured surface and lightly knead until smooth. Roll out to 2cm/¾in thick and stamp out nine scones with a floured 6cm/2½in cookie cutter.

4 Transfer to a non-stick baking sheet. Brush with skimmed milk, then sprinkle over the cayenne pepper. Bake for 15 minutes, until golden brown. Serve warm or cold.

Wholemeal Herb Triangles

Stuffed with cooked chicken and salad, these make a good lunchtime snack, and are also an ideal accompaniment to a bowl of steaming soup.

Makes 8

INGREDIENTS

225g/8oz/2 cups wholemeal plain flour
115g/4oz/1 cup strong plain flour
pinch of salt
2.5ml/½ tsp bicarbonate of soda
5ml/1 tsp cream of tartar
2.5ml/½ tsp chilli powder
50g/2oz/¼ cup margarine, chopped
60ml/4 tbsp chopped mixed fresh herbs
250ml/8fl oz/1 cup skimmed milk
15ml/1 tbsp sesame seeds

1 Preheat the oven to 220°C/425°F/Gas 7. Lightly flour a baking sheet. Put the wholemeal flour in a mixing bowl. Sift in the salt, bicarbonate of soda, cream of tartar and chilli powder, then rub in the margarine.

2 Add the herbs and milk and mix quickly to a soft dough. Turn on to a lightly floured surface. Knead only very briefly or the dough will become tough.

3 Roll the dough out to a 23cm/9in round and place on the prepared baking sheet. Brush lightly with water and sprinkle the top evenly with the sesame seeds.

4 Carefully cut the dough round into eight wedges, separate them slightly and bake for 15–20 minutes. Transfer to a wire rack to cool. Serve warm or cold.

Variation To make Sun-dried Tomato Triangles, replace the fresh mixed herbs with 30ml/2 tbsp drained chopped sun-dried tomatoes in oil and add 15ml/1 tbsp each mild paprika, chopped fresh parsley and chopped fresh marjoram.

Dill and Potato Cakes

Makes 10

INGREDIENTS

225g/8oz/2 cups self-raising flour
40g/1½oz/3 tbsp butter
pinch of salt
15ml/1 tbsp finely chopped fresh dill
175g/6oz/scant 1 cup mashed potato, freshly made
30–45ml/2–3 tbsp milk

1 Preheat the oven to 230°C/450°F/Gas 8. Sift the flour into a bowl, and add the butter, salt and dill. Mix in the potato and enough milk to make a soft dough.

2 Roll out the dough until fairly thin. Cut into neat rounds with a floured 7.5cm/3in cutter. Place the cakes on a greased baking sheet, and bake for 20–25 minutes.

Chive and Potato Scones

These little scones should be fairly thin, soft and crisp on the outside. Serve them for breakfast.

Makes 20

INGREDIENTS

450g/1lb potatoes
115g/4oz/1 cup plain flour
30ml/2 tbsp olive oil
30ml/2 tbsp snipped chives
salt and black pepper

Cook's Tip Cook the scones over a constant low heat so that the outsides do not burn before the insides are cooked through.

1 Cook the potatoes in a saucepan of boiling salted water for 20 minutes, until tender, then drain thoroughly. Return the potatoes to the clean pan and mash them. Preheat a griddle or heavy frying pan.

2 Add the flour, olive oil, chives and a little salt and pepper to the mashed potato. Mix to a soft dough.

3 Roll out the dough on a well-floured surface to a thickness of 5mm/¼in and stamp out rounds with a floured 5cm/2in plain pastry cutter. Lightly grease the griddle or frying pan.

4 Cook the scones for about 10 minutes, turning once.

Curry Crackers

These spicy, crisp little biscuits are ideal for serving with drinks.

Makes 12

INGREDIENTS

50g/2oz/½ cup plain flour
pinch of salt
5ml/1 tsp curry powder
1.5ml/¼ tsp chilli powder
15ml/1 tbsp chopped fresh coriander
30ml/2 tbsp water

1 Preheat the oven to 180°C/350°F/Gas 4. Sift the flour and salt into a mixing bowl, then add the curry powder and chilli powder. Make a well in the centre and add the chopped fresh coriander and water. Gradually incorporate the flour and mix to a firm dough.

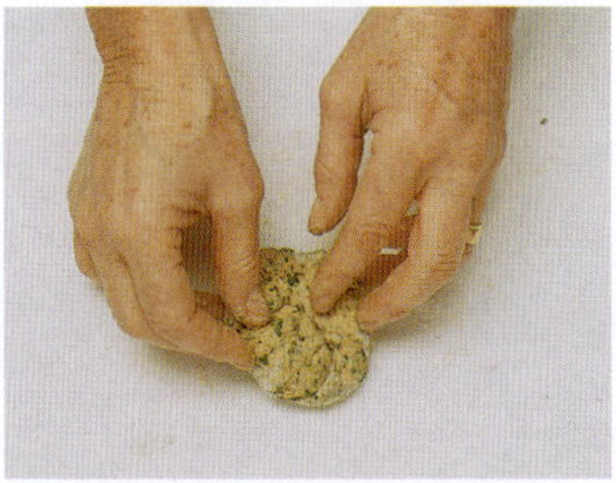

2 Turn the dough on to a lightly floured surface, knead until smooth, then leave to rest for 5 minutes.

3 Cut the dough into 12 even-size pieces and knead into small balls. Roll each ball out very thinly to a 10cm/4in round, sprinkling more flour over the dough if necessary to prevent it from sticking to the rolling pin.

4 Arrange the rounds on two ungreased baking sheets, then bake for 15 minutes, turning over once during cooking. Transfer to a wire rack to cool.

Cocktail Shapes

Tiny savoury biscuits are always a welcome treat. Try using different flavours and shapes.

Makes 80

INGREDIENTS

350g/12oz/3 cups plain flour
pinch of salt
2.5ml/½ tsp black pepper
5ml/1 tsp whole grain mustard
175g/6oz/¾ cup butter, chopped
115g/4oz Cheddar cheese
1 egg, beaten
5ml/1 tsp chopped nuts
10ml/2 tsp dill seeds
10ml/2 tsp curry paste
10ml/2 tsp chilli sauce

1 Preheat the oven to 200°C/400°F/ Gas 6. Line several baking sheets with non-stick baking paper. Sift the flour into a mixing bowl and add the salt, pepper and mustard.

2 Rub the butter into the flour mixture until it resembles fine breadcrumbs. Grate the cheese then with a fork stir it into the butter and flour mixture. Add the egg, and mix together to form a soft dough.

3 Knead lightly on a floured surface and cut into four equal pieces.

4 Knead chopped nuts into one piece, dill seeds into another piece and curry paste and chilli sauce into each of the remaining pieces. Wrap each piece of flavoured dough in clear film and chill for at least 1 hour. Remove from the clear film and roll out one piece at a time.

5 Using a floured heart-shaped cutter, stamp out about 20 shapes from the curry-flavoured dough and use a club-shaped cutter to cut out the chilli-flavoured dough. Arrange the shapes well spaced apart on the prepared baking sheets and bake in the oven for 6–8 minutes, until slightly puffed and pale gold in colour. Cool on wire racks.

6 Repeat with the remaining flavoured dough using spade- and diamond-shaped cutters. Knead any trimmings together, re-roll and stamp out and bake as above.

Spiced Cocktail Biscuits

These savoury biscuits are ideal for serving with pre-dinner drinks. Each of the spice seeds contributes to the flavour.

Makes 20–30

INGREDIENTS

150g/5oz/1¼ cups plain flour
10ml/2 tsp curry powder
115g/4oz/½ cup butter, chopped
75g/3oz/¾ cup grated Cheddar cheese,
10ml/2 tsp poppy seeds
5ml/1 tsp black onion seeds
1 egg yolk
cumin seeds, to garnish

Variation Use caraway or sesame seeds instead of the poppy seeds if you wish.

1 Grease two baking sheets. Sift the flour and curry powder into a large bowl. Rub in the butter until the mixture resembles breadcrumbs, then stir in the cheese, poppy seeds and black onion seeds. Stir in the egg yolk and mix to a firm dough. Wrap the dough in clear film and chill for 30 minutes.

2 Roll out the dough on a floured surface to a thickness of about 3mm/⅛in. Cut into rounds with a floured cookie cutter. Arrange on the prepared baking sheets and sprinkle with the cumin seeds. Chill for 15 minutes.

3 Preheat the oven to 190°C/375°F/ Gas 5. Bake for approximately 20 minutes, until crisp and golden. Serve warm or cold.

Brownies and Bars

A brownie should be a moist, chewy bar, crisp on the outside but as if underdone inside. There are many recipes for brownies, varying in richness.

Bars are the quickest and easiest cookies to shape evenly. The cookie mixture is simply poured or pressed into the tin, baked, then cut to the required size with a large, sharp knife while still warm from the oven.

Some bar cookies are just a single layer, while others are double- or even triple-layered. The layers are sometimes added before baking, sometimes part of the way through the cooking, depending on the recipe.

Try to use the size of tin stated in a recipe. If you use one that is smaller, the layer of mixture will be deeper so the outside of the bars will become overcooked and too brown and crisp or hard before the inside is ready, whereas if too large a tin is used the mixture will be spread too thinly, and not only will it cook too quickly and dry out, but the ratio of centre to outside crust will be adversely affected. If you only have a larger tin, the size can be reduced by making a wide strip formed from a triple thickness of foil to fit across the tin at the right place. Fold up along a long edge to make a lap that the weight of the mixture will hold down, keeping the foil divider in place.

Bar cookies can be stored for a day or so in their baking tin. Cover the tin as tightly as you can with foil, or slide it into a plastic bag, gently press out as much air as possible and seal tightly.

White Chocolate Brownies

Makes 16

INGREDIENTS

150g/5oz/1¼ cups plain flour
2.5ml/½ tsp baking powder
pinch of salt
175g/6oz fine quality white chocolate, chopped
90g/3½oz/½ cup caster sugar
115g/4oz/½ cup unsalted butter, chopped
2 eggs, lightly beaten
5ml/1 tsp vanilla essence
175g/6oz plain chocolate, chopped, or plain chocolate chips
For the topping
200g/7oz milk chocolate, chopped
215g/7½oz/2 cups unsalted macadamia nuts, chopped

1 Preheat the oven to 180°C/350°F/Gas 4. Grease a 23cm/9in springform tin. Sift together the flour, baking powder and salt. Set aside.

2 In a medium saucepan over medium heat, melt the white chocolate, sugar and butter, stirring until smooth.

3 Cool slightly, then beat in the eggs and vanilla essence. Stir in the flour until well blended. Stir in the chopped chocolate or chocolate chips. Spread evenly in the prepared tin, smoothing the top.

4 Bake for 20–25 minutes until a skewer inserted 5cm/2in from the side of the tin comes out clean. Remove from the oven. Sprinkle chopped milk chocolate evenly over the surface (avoid touching the side of tin) and return to oven for 1 minute.

5 Remove from the oven and, using the back of a spoon, spread the softened chocolate evenly over the top. Sprinkle with the macadamia nuts and gently press into the chocolate. Cool on a wire rack for 30 minutes, then chill until set. Run a sharp knife around the side of the tin to loosen; unclip the tin side and carefully remove. Cut into thin wedges.

Marbled Brownies

Makes 24

INGREDIENTS

225g/8oz plain chocolate, chopped
75g/3oz/⅓ cup butter, chopped
4 eggs
350g/12oz/1½ cups caster sugar
115g/4oz/1 cup plain flour
pinch of salt
5ml/1 tsp baking powder
10ml/2 tsp vanilla essence
115g/4oz/1 cup walnuts, chopped
For the plain batter
50g/2oz/4 tbsp butter
175g/6oz/⅔ cup cream cheese
115g/4oz/½ cup caster sugar
2 eggs
30ml/2 tbsp plain flour
5ml/1 tsp vanilla essence

1 Preheat the oven to 180°C/350°F/Gas 4. Line a 33 x 23 cm/13 x 9in tin with greaseproof paper and grease the paper.

2 Melt the chocolate and butter in a saucepan over a very low heat.

3 Meanwhile, beat the eggs until light and fluffy. Gradually add the sugar and continue beating until blended. Sift over the flour, salt and baking powder and fold in.

4 Stir in the cooled chocolate mixture, and the vanilla essence and walnuts. Set aside 475ml/16fl oz/2 cups of the chocolate batter.

5 To make the plain batter, cream the butter and cream cheese with an electric mixer.

6 Add the sugar and continue beating until blended. Beat in the eggs, flour and vanilla essence.

7 Spread the unmeasured chocolate batter into the tin. Pour over the cream cheese mixture. Drop spoonfuls of the reserved chocolate batter on top.

8 With a metal spatula, swirl the mixtures to marble. Do not blend completely. Bake for 35–40 minutes, until just set. Unmould when cool and cut into squares for serving.

Fudgy Glazed Chocolate Slices

Makes 8–10

INGREDIENTS

300g/11oz plain chocolate, chopped
115g/4oz/½ cup unsalted butter, chopped
90g/3½oz/generous ½ cup light brown sugar
50g/2oz/¼ cup granulated sugar
2 eggs
15ml/1 tbsp vanilla essence
65g/2½oz/½ cup plain flour
115g/4oz/1 cup pecans or walnuts, toasted and chopped
150g/5oz fine quality white chocolate, chopped
For the Fudgy Chocolate Glaze
175g/6oz plain chocolate, chopped
50g/2oz/4 tbsp unsalted butter, chopped
30ml/2 tbsp golden syrup
10ml/2 tsp vanilla essence
5ml/1 tsp instant coffee powder
pecan halves, to decorate (optional)

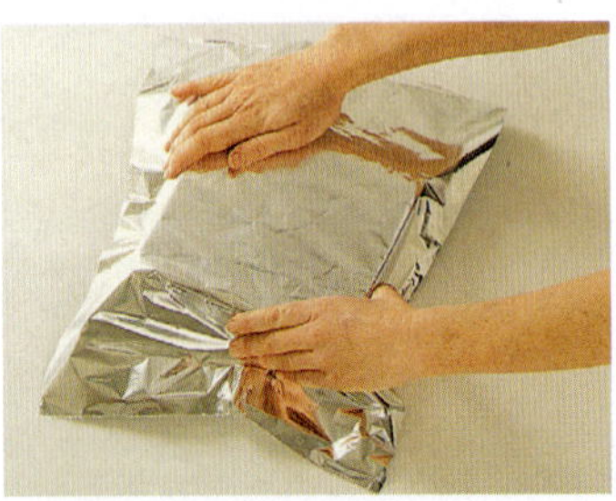

1 Preheat the oven to 180°C/350°F/Gas 4. Invert a 20cm/8in square baking tin and mould a piece of foil over the bottom. Turn the tin over and line with moulded foil. Lightly grease the foil.

2 In a medium saucepan over a low heat, melt the plain chocolate and butter, stirring until smooth.

3 Stir in the sugars and continue stirring for 2 minutes, until the sugar has dissolved. Beat in the eggs and vanilla essence. Stir in the flour, nuts and white chocolate. Pour the batter into the prepared tin.

4 Bake for 20–25 minutes, until a skewer inserted 5cm/2in from the centre comes out clean. Remove the tin to a wire rack to cool for 30 minutes. Using the foil, lift from the tin and cool on the wire rack for 2 hours.

5 To make the glaze, melt the chocolate, butter, syrup, vanilla essence and coffee powder in a medium saucepan over a medium heat, stirring frequently, until smooth. Remove from the heat. Chill for 1 hour, until thickened and spreadable.

6 Invert the cake on to the wire rack, remove the foil from the bottom. Turn top side up. Using a metal palette knife, spread a thick layer of fudgy glaze over the top of the cake just to the edges. Chill for 1 hour, until set. Cut into squares or fingers. If you wish, top each with a pecan half.

Chocolate Brownies

Traditional American brownies are usually rich in fat. This no-butter version still tastes dark and gooey, but is best eaten on the day it is made.

Makes 20

INGREDIENTS

120ml/4fl oz/½ cup sunflower oil
150g/5oz plain chocolate, chopped
2 eggs
115g/4oz/1 cup self-raising flour
115g/4oz/½ cup caster sugar
5ml/1 tsp vanilla essence
75g/3oz/¾ cup halved pecans

1 Preheat the oven to 200°C/400°F/ Gas 6. Use a little of the oil to grease a 23cm/9in square shallow cake tin and line with lightly oiled greaseproof paper.

Cook's Tip Ingredients can be melted easily in the microwave. To soften chocolate, butter, sugar or syrup, microwave on full power for a few minutes, until soft.

2 Melt the chocolate with the remaining oil in a heatproof bowl over a saucepan of water, stirring until smooth.

3 Beat the eggs lightly and add them to the chocolate, stirring vigorously. Beat in the flour, sugar and vanilla essence and pour the mixture into the prepared tin. Arrange the pecans over the top.

4 Bake for 10–15 minutes. If you like chewy brownies, take them out of the oven now. If you want a more cake-like finish, leave for another 5 minutes. Cut into squares and leave to cool before removing from the tin.

Nut and Chocolate Chip Brownies

These brownies are moist, dark and deeply satisfying.

Makes 16

INGREDIENTS

150g/5oz plain chocolate, chopped
120ml/4fl oz/½ cup sunflower oil
215g/7½oz/1¼ cups light muscovado sugar
2 eggs
5ml/1 tsp vanilla essence
65g/2½oz/⅔ cup self-raising flour
60ml/4 tbsp cocoa powder
75g/3oz/¾ cup chopped walnuts or pecans
60ml/4 tbsp milk chocolate chips

Cook's Tip These brownies will freeze for 3 months in an airtight container.

1 Preheat the oven to 180°C/350°F/Gas 4. Lightly grease a shallow 19cm/7½in square cake tin. Melt the plain chocolate in a heatproof bowl over a saucepan of hot water.

2 With an electric whisk, beat the oil, sugar, eggs and vanilla essence together in a large bowl.

3 Stir in the melted chocolate, then beat well until evenly mixed.

4 Sift the flour and cocoa powder into the bowl and fold in thoroughly. Stir in the chopped nuts and chocolate chips, tip into the prepared tin and spread evenly to the edges. Bake for 30–35 minutes, until the top is firm and crusty. Cool in the tin before cutting into squares.

Banana Ginger Parkin

Parkin keeps well and actually improves with keeping. Store it in a covered container for up to 2 months.

Makes 26

INGREDIENTS

200g/7oz/1¾ cups plain flour
10ml/2 tsp bicarbonate of soda
10ml/2 tsp ground ginger
150g/5oz/1¾ cups medium oatmeal
60ml/4 tbsp dark muscovado sugar
75g/3oz/⅓ cup sunflower margarine, chopped
150g/5oz/⅔ cup golden syrup
1 egg, beaten
3 ripe bananas, mashed
75g/3oz/¾ cup icing sugar
stem ginger, to decorate

Cook's Tip These are nutritious, energy-giving squares that are a really good choice for packed lunches as they don't break up too easily.

1 Preheat the oven to 160°C/325°F/Gas 3. Grease and line an 18 x 28cm/7 x 11in cake tin.

2 Sift together the flour, bicarbonate of soda and ginger, then stir in the oatmeal. Melt the sugar, margarine and syrup in a saucepan over a low heat, then stir into the flour mixture. Beat in the egg and mashed bananas.

3 Spoon into the prepared tin and bake for about 1 hour, until firm to the touch. Leave to cool in the tin, then turn out and cut into squares.

4 Sift the icing sugar into a bowl and stir in just enough water to make a smooth, runny icing. Drizzle the icing over each square and top with a piece of stem ginger.

Parkin Squares

The flavour of these squares will improve if they are stored in an airtight container for several days or a week before serving.

Makes 16–20

INGREDIENTS

300ml/½ pint/1¼ cups milk
225g/8oz/¾ cup golden syrup
225g/8oz/¾ cup black treacle
115g/4oz/½ cup butter or margarine, chopped
50g/2oz/⅓ cup dark brown sugar
450g/1lb/4 cups plain flour
2.5ml/½ tsp bicarbonate of soda
6.25ml/1¼ tsp ground ginger
350g/12oz/4 cups medium oatmeal
1 egg, beaten
icing sugar for dusting

1 Preheat the oven to 180°C/350°F/Gas 4. Grease and line the base of a 20cm/8in square cake tin. Gently heat together the milk, syrup, treacle, butter or margarine and sugar, stirring until smooth; do not boil.

2 Stir together the flour, bicarbonate of soda, ginger and oatmeal. Make a well in the centre, pour in the egg, then slowly pour in the warmed mixture, stirring to make a smooth batter.

3 Pour the batter into the tin and bake for about 45 minutes, until firm to the touch. Cool slightly in the tin, then cool completely on a wire rack. Cut into squares and dust with icing sugar.

Chocolate Pecan Squares

Makes 16

INGREDIENTS

2 eggs
10ml/2 tsp vanilla essence
pinch of salt
175g/6oz/1½ cups pecans, coarsely chopped
50g/2oz/½ cup plain flour
50g/2oz/4 tbsp granulated sugar
175g/6oz/½ cup treacle
75g/3oz/3 x 1oz plain chocolate, finely chopped
45g/1½oz/3 tbsp butter
16 pecan halves for decorating

1 Preheat the oven to 160°C/325°F/Gas 3. Line the bottom and sides of a 20cm/8in square baking tin with paper and grease lightly.

2 Whisk together the eggs, vanilla essence and salt. In another bowl, mix together the pecans and flour. Set both bowls aside.

3 In a saucepan, bring the sugar and treacle to a boil.

4 Remove from the heat and stir in the chocolate and butter and blend thoroughly with a wooden spoon.

5 Mix in the beaten eggs, then fold in the pecan mixture. Pour the batter into the prepared tin and bake for about 35 minutes, until set.

6 Cool in the tin for 10 minutes before unmoulding. Cut into 5cm/2in squares and press pecan halves into the tops while warm. Cool completely on a wire rack.

Raisin Brownies

Makes 16

INGREDIENTS

115g/4oz/½ cup butter or margarine, chopped
50g/2oz/½ cup cocoa powder
2 eggs
225g/8oz/1 cup caster sugar
5ml/1 tsp vanilla essence
40g/1½oz/⅓ cup plain flour
75g/3oz/¾ cup walnuts, chopped
65g/2½oz/½ cup raisins

1 Preheat the oven to 180°C/350°F/Gas 4. Line a 20cm/8in square baking tin with greaseproof paper and grease the paper.

2 Melt the butter or margarine in a small saucepan over a low heat. Remove from the heat and stir in the cocoa powder.

3 With an electric mixer, beat together the eggs, sugar, and vanilla essence until light. Add the cocoa mixture and stir to blend.

4 Sift the flour over the cocoa mixture and gently fold in. Add the walnuts and raisins and scrape the batter into the prepared tin. Bake for 30 minutes. Do not overbake.

5 Leave in the tin to cool before cutting into 5cm/2in squares and removing. The brownies should be soft and moist. Dust with icing sugar before serving.

Chocolate Butterscotch Bars

Makes 24

INGREDIENTS

225g/8oz/2 cups plain flour
2.5ml/½ tsp baking powder
115g/4oz/½ cup unsalted butter, chopped
50g/2oz/⅓ cup light muscovado sugar
150g/5oz plain chocolate, melted
30ml/2 tbsp ground almonds
For the topping
175g/6oz/¾ cup unsalted butter
115g/4oz/½ cup caster sugar
30ml/2 tbsp golden syrup
175ml/6fl oz/¾ cup condensed milk
150g/5oz/1¼ cups whole toasted hazelnuts
225g/8oz plain chocolate, chopped

1 Preheat the oven to 160°C/325°F/Gas 3. Grease a shallow 30 x 20cm/12 x 8in cake tin. Sift the flour and baking powder into a large bowl. Rub in the butter then stir in the sugar. Work in the melted chocolate and ground almonds.

2 Press the mixture into the prepared cake tin, prick the surface with a fork and bake for 25–30 minutes, until firm. Leave to cool.

3 To make the topping, mix the butter, sugar, golden syrup and condensed milk in a saucepan. Heat gently until the butter and sugar have melted. Simmer, stirring occasionally, until golden, then stir in the hazelnuts.

4 Pour over the cooked base and spread out evenly. Leave to set.

5 Melt the chocolate in a bowl over a saucepan of hot water. Spread over the butterscotch layer; leave to set before cutting into bars.

Soured Cream Streusel Bars

A deliciously different tea-time treat.

Makes 12–14

INGREDIENTS

115g/4oz/½ cup butter
150g/5oz/⅔ cup granulated sugar
3 eggs, at room temperature
175g/6oz/1½ cups plain flour
5ml/1 tsp bicarbonate of soda
5ml/1 tsp baking powder
250ml/8fl oz/1 cup soured cream
For the topping
175g/6oz/1 firmly packed cup dark brown sugar
10ml/2 tsp ground cinnamon
115g/4oz/1 cup walnuts, finely chopped
50g/2oz/4 tbsp butter, chopped

1 Preheat the oven to 180°C/350°F/Gas 4. Line the bottom of a 23cm/9in square cake tin with greaseproof paper and grease the paper.

2 To make the topping, place the brown sugar, cinnamon and walnuts in a bowl. Mix with your fingertips, then add the butter and continue working until the mixture resembles coarse crumbs.

3 Cream the butter with an electric mixer until soft. Add the sugar and continue beating until the mixture is light and fluffy.

4 Add the eggs, one at a time, beating well after each addition.

5 In another bowl, sift the flour, bicarbonate of soda and baking powder together three times.

6 Fold the dry ingredients into the butter mixture in three batches, alternating with the soured cream. Fold until blended after each addition.

7 Pour half of the batter into the prepared tin and sprinkle over half of the topping.

8 Pour the remaining batter on top and sprinkle over the remaining topping.

9 Bake for 60–70 minutes, until browned. Leave to stand for 5 minutes, then unmould and transfer to a wire rack to cool.

White Chocolate Macadamia Slices

Keep these luxury slices for someone special who will really appreciate their superb rich flavour and crunchy texture.

Makes 16

INGREDIENTS

150g/5oz/1¼ cups macadamia nuts, blanched almonds or hazelnuts
400g/14oz white chocolate, chopped
50g/2oz/⅓ cup ready-to-eat dried apricots
75g/3oz/⅓ cup unsalted butter
5ml/1 tsp vanilla essence
3 eggs
150g/5oz/scant 1 cup light muscovado sugar
115g/4oz/1 cup self-raising flour

1 Preheat the oven to 190°C/375°F/Gas 5. Lightly grease two 20cm/8in sandwich cake tins and line the base of each with greaseproof paper or non-stick baking paper.

2 Roughly chop the nuts and half the white chocolate, making sure that the pieces are more or less the same size, then cut up the apricots to similar-size pieces.

3 In the top of a double boiler or in a heatproof bowl over a saucepan of hot water, melt the remaining white chocolate over a gentle heat with the butter, stirring occasionally until smooth. Remove the bowl from the heat.

4 Stir in the vanilla essence. Whisk the eggs and sugar in a mixing bowl until thick and pale, then whisk in the melted chocolate mixture.

5 Sift the flour over the mixture and fold it in evenly. Stir in the nuts, white chocolate and apricots.

6 Spoon the mixture into the prepared tins and smooth the top level with a spatula and bake for 30–35 minutes.

Cook's Tip You might find it easier to use sharp kitchen scissors rather than a knife to snip the apricots into small pieces.

Toffee Bars

Makes 32

INGREDIENTS

350g/12oz/2 cups light brown sugar
450g/1lb/2 cups butter or margarine
2 egg yolks
7.5ml/1½ tsp vanilla essence
450g/1lb/4 cups plain or wholemeal flour
pinch of salt
225g/8oz milk chocolate, chopped
115g/4oz/1 cup walnuts, chopped

1 Preheat the oven to 180°C/350°F/ Gas 4. Grease a 33 x 23 x 5cm/ 13 x 9 x 2in cake tin. Beat together the sugar and butter or margarine until light and fluffy. Beat in the egg yolks and vanilla essence. Stir in the flour and salt.

2 Spread the dough in the prepared cake tin. Bake for 25–30 minutes, until lightly browned. The texture will be soft.

3 Remove from the oven and immediately place the chocolate pieces on the hot cookie base. Leave to stand until the chocolate softens, then spread it evenly with a spatula. Sprinkle with the nuts. While still warm, cut into about 5 x 4cm/2 x 1½in bars.

Variation Use chopped pecan nuts instead of walnuts if you prefer, or try a mixture of both.

Chocolate Walnut Bars

Makes 24

INGREDIENTS

50g/2oz/½ cup walnuts
75g/3oz/⅓ cup granulated sugar
75g/3oz/¾ cup plain flour, sifted
75g/3oz/6 tbsp cold unsalted butter, chopped
For the topping
25g/1oz/2 tbsp unsalted butter
75g/3oz/⅓ cup water
40g/1½oz/⅓ cup cocoa powder
115g/4oz/½ cup granulated sugar
5ml/1 tsp vanilla essence
pinch of salt
2 eggs
icing sugar for dusting

1 Preheat the oven to 180°C/350°F/ Gas 4. Grease the sides and bottom of a 20cm/8in square cake tin.

2 Grind the walnuts with a few tablespoons of the sugar in a food processor, blender or nut grinder.

3 In a bowl, combine the ground walnuts, the remaining sugar, and the flour. Rub in the butter until the mixture resembles coarse crumbs. Alternatively, put all the ingredients in a food processor and process until the mixture resembles coarse crumbs.

4 Pat the walnut mixture into the bottom of the prepared tin in an even layer. Bake for 25 minutes.

5 Meanwhile, to make the topping, melt the butter with the water in a small saucepan over a low heat. Whisk in the cocoa and sugar.

6 Remove the pan from the heat, stir in the vanilla essence and salt and leave to cool for 5 minutes.

7 Whisk in the eggs until blended. Pour the topping evenly over the crust when it is cooked.

8 Return to the oven and bake for about 20 minutes until set. Set the tin on a wire rack to cool. Cut into 7 x 2.5cm/2½ x 1in bars and dust with icing sugar. Store in the refrigerator.

Pecan Squares

Makes 36

INGREDIENTS

225g/8oz/2 cups plain flour
pinch of salt
115g/4oz/½ cup granulated sugar
225g/8oz/1 cup cold butter or margarine, chopped
1 egg
finely grated rind of 1 lemon
For the topping
175g/6oz/¾ cup butter
75g/3oz/¼ cup honey
50g/2oz/¼ cup granulated sugar
115g/4oz/½ firmly packed cup dark brown sugar
75ml/5 tbsp whipping cream
450g/1lb/4 cups pecan halves

1 Preheat the oven to 190°C/375°F/Gas 5. Lightly grease a 37 x 27 x 2.5cm/15½ x 10½ x 1in Swiss roll tin.

2 Sift the flour and salt into a mixing bowl. Stir in the sugar. Cut and rub in the butter or margarine until the mixture resembles coarse crumbs. Add the egg and lemon rind and blend with a fork until the mixture just holds together.

3 Spoon the mixture into the prepared tin. With floured fingertips, press into an even layer. Prick the pastry all over with a fork and chill for 10 minutes.

4 Bake the pastry crust for 15 minutes. Remove the tin from the oven, but keep the oven on while making the topping.

5 To make the topping, melt the butter, honey and both sugars. Bring to the boil. Boil, without stirring, for 2 minutes. Off the heat, stir in the cream and pecans. Pour over the crust, return to the oven and bake for 25 minutes. Leave to cool.

6 When cool, run a knife around the edge. Invert on to a baking sheet, place another sheet on top and invert again. Dip a sharp knife into very hot water and cut into squares for serving.

Hazelnut Squares

Makes 9

INGREDIENTS

50g/2oz plain chocolate, chopped
65g/2½oz/⅓ cup butter or margarine
225g/8oz/1 cup caster sugar
50g/2oz/½ cup plain flour
2.5ml/½ tsp baking powder
2 eggs, beaten
2.5ml/½ tsp vanilla essence
115g/4oz/1 cup skinned hazelnuts, roughly chopped

1 Preheat the oven to 180°C/350°F/Gas 4. Grease a 20cm/8in square cake tin.

2 In a heatproof bowl set over a saucepan of hot water, melt the chocolate and butter or margarine, stirring until smooth.

3 Add the sugar, flour, baking powder, eggs, vanilla essence and half of the hazelnuts to the mixture and stir with a wooden spoon.

4 Pour the mixture into the prepared cake tin. Bake for 10 minutes, then sprinkle the remaining hazelnuts over the top. Return to the oven and continue baking for about 25 minutes, until firm to the touch.

5 Leave to cool in the tin, set on a wire rack, for 10 minutes, then transfer to the rack and leave to cool completely. Cut into squares for serving.

Almond-topped Squares

Makes 18

INGREDIENTS

75g/3oz/6 tbsp butter
50g/2oz/¼ cup granulated sugar
1 egg yolk
grated rind and juice of ½ lemon
2.5ml/½ tsp vanilla essence
30ml/2 tbsp whipping cream
115g/4oz/1 cup plain flour
For the topping
225g/8oz/1 cup granulated sugar
75g/3oz/¾ cup sliced almonds
4 egg whites
2.5ml/½ tsp ground ginger
2.5ml/½ tsp ground cinnamon

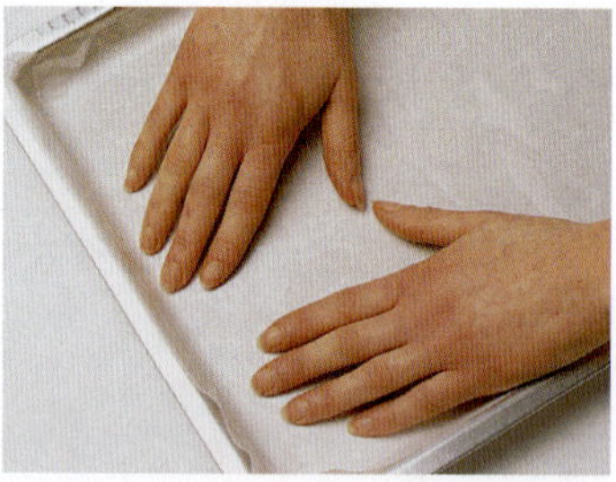

1 Preheat the oven to 190°C/375°F/ Gas 5. Line a 33 x 23cm/13 x 9in Swiss roll tin with greaseproof paper and grease the paper.

2 With an electric mixer, cream the butter and sugar until light and fluffy. Beat in the egg yolk, lemon rind and juice, the vanilla essence and cream.

3 Gradually stir in the flour. Gather into a ball of dough. With lightly floured fingers, press the dough into the prepared tin. Bake for 15 minutes. Remove from the oven but leave the oven on.

4 To make the topping, combine all the ingredients in a heavy saucepan. Cook, stirring until the mixture comes to the boil. Boil for 1 minute. Pour over the dough, spreading evenly.

5 Return to the oven and bake for about 45 minutes. Remove and score into bars or squares.

Lemon Squares

Makes 12

INGREDIENTS

225g/8oz/2 cups plain flour
50g/2oz/½ cup icing sugar
pinch of salt
175g/6oz/¾ cup butter or margarine
5ml/1 tsp cold water
For the lemon layer
4 eggs
450g/1lb/2 cups caster sugar
25g/1oz/2 tbsp plain flour
2.5ml/½ tsp baking powder
5ml/1 tsp grated lemon rind
50ml/2fl oz/¼ cup fresh lemon juice
icing sugar for sprinkling

1 Preheat the oven to 180°C/350°F/Gas 4. Sift the flour, icing sugar and salt into a mixing bowl.

2 Rub the butter or margarine into the flour until the mixture resembles coarse breadcrumbs. Add the water and toss lightly with a fork until the mixture forms a ball.

3 Press the mixture evenly into an ungreased 33 x 23cm/13 x 9in baking dish. Bake for 15–20 minutes, until light golden brown. Remove from the oven and leave to cool slightly.

4 Meanwhile, to make the lemon layer, beat together the eggs, caster sugar, flour, baking powder and lemon rind and juice.

5 Pour the lemon mixture over the baked dish. Return to the oven and bake for 25 minutes. Leave to cool in the baking dish, placed on a wire rack.

6 Before serving, sprinkle the top with icing sugar. Cut into squares with a sharp knife.

Apricot and Almond Fingers

These apricot and almond fingers will stay moist for several days.

Makes 18

INGREDIENTS

225g/8oz/2 cups self-raising flour
115g/4oz/²/₃ cup light muscovado sugar
50g/2oz/¹/₃ cup semolina
175g/6oz/1 cup ready-to-use dried apricots, chopped
2 eggs
30ml/2 tbsp malt extract
30ml/2 tbsp clear honey
60ml/4 tbsp skimmed milk
60ml/4 tbsp sunflower oil
few drops of almond essence
30ml/2 tbsp flaked almonds

1 Preheat the oven to 160°C/325°F/ Gas 3. Lightly grease and line a 28 x 18cm/11 x 7in shallow cake tin. Sift the flour into a bowl and add the muscovado sugar, semolina, dried apricots and eggs. Add the malt extract, clear honey, milk, sunflower oil and almond essence. Mix well until smooth.

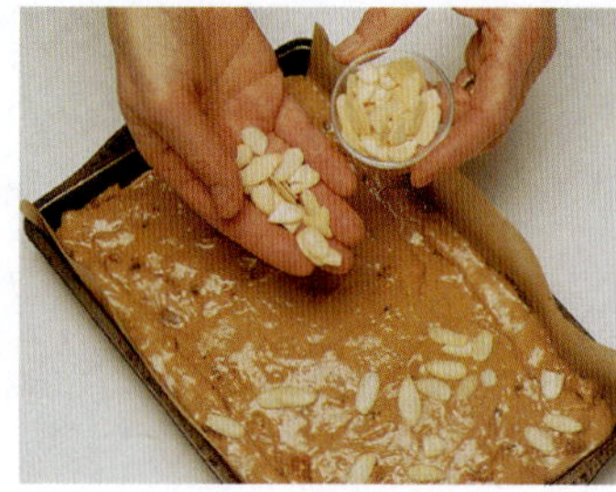

2 Turn the mixture into the prepared cake tin, spread to the edges and sprinkle with the flaked almonds.

3 Bake for 30–35 minutes, until the centre of the cake springs back when lightly pressed. Transfer to a wire rack to cool. Remove the paper, place the cake on a board and cut it into18 slices with a sharp knife.

Apricot Bars

Makes 12

INGREDIENTS

75g/3oz/½ cup firmly packed light brown sugar
75g/3oz/¾ cup flour
75g/3oz/⅓ cup cold unsalted butter, chopped
For the topping
175g/6oz/1 cup dried apricots
250ml/8fl oz/1 cup water
grated rind of 1 lemon
75g/3oz/⅓ cup granulated sugar
10ml/2 tsp cornflour
50g/2oz/½ cup walnuts, chopped

1 Preheat the oven to 180°C/350°F/Gas 4. Grease a 20cm/8in square cake tin.

2 In a bowl, combine the sugar and flour. Rub in the butter until the mixture resembles coarse crumbs.

3 Press into the prepared cake tin. Bake for 15 minutes. Remove from the oven but leave the oven on.

4 To make the topping, combine the apricots and water in a saucepan and simmer for about 10 minutes, until soft. Strain the liquid and reserve. Chop the apricots.

5 Return the apricots to the saucepan and add the lemon rind, granulated sugar, cornflour, and 60ml/4 tbsp of the soaking liquid. Cook for 1 minute.

6 Cool slightly before spreading the topping over the base. Sprinkle over the walnuts and continue baking for 20 minutes more. Leave to cool in the tin before cutting into bars.

Blueberry Streusel Slices

Makes 30

INGREDIENTS

225g/8oz shortcrust pastry
50g/2oz/1/2 cup plain flour
1.5ml/1/4 tsp baking powder
40g/1 1/2oz/3 tbsp butter or margarine
25g/1oz/2 tbsp fresh white breadcrumbs
50g/2oz/1/3 cup soft light brown sugar
pinch of salt
50g/2oz/4 tbsp flaked or chopped almonds
60ml/4 tbsp blackberry or bramble jelly
115g/4oz/scant 1 cup blueberries, fresh or frozen

1 Preheat the oven to 180°C/350°F/Gas 4. Roll out the pastry on a lightly floured surface to fit an 18 x 28cm/7 x 11in Swiss roll tin. Grease the Swiss roll tin.

2 Rub together the flour, baking powder, butter or margarine, breadcrumbs, sugar and salt until really crumbly, then mix in the almonds.

3 Place the rolled pastry in the prepared tin. Spread the pastry with the jelly, sprinkle with the blueberries, then cover evenly with the streusel topping, pressing down lightly. Bake for 30–40 minutes, lowering the temperature after 20 minutes to 160°C/325°F/Gas 3.

4 Remove from the oven. Cut into slices while still hot, then transfer to a wire rack to cool.

Sticky Date and Apple Squares

If possible, allow this mixture to mature for 1–2 days before cutting.

Makes 16

INGREDIENTS

115g/4oz/1/2 cup margarine
50g/2oz/4 tbsp soft dark brown sugar
50g/2oz/4 tbsp golden syrup
115g/4oz/2/3 cup chopped dates
115g/4oz/1 1/3 cup rolled oats
115g/4oz/1 cup wholemeal self-raising flour
2 eating apples, peeled, cored and grated
5–10ml/1–2 tsp lemon juice
walnut halves

1 Preheat the oven to 190°C/375°F/Gas 5. Line an 18–20cm/7–8in square or rectangle loose-based cake tin. In a large saucepan, gently heat the margarine, sugar and syrup together until the margarine has melted completely.

2 Add the dates and cook until they have softened. Gradually work in the oats, flour, apples and lemon juice until well mixed.

3 Spoon into the prepared tin and spread out evenly. Top with the walnut halves. Bake for 30 minutes, then reduce the temperature to 160°C/325°F/ Gas 3 and bake for 10–12 minutes more, until firm to the touch and golden.

4 Cut into squares or bars while still warm if you are going to eat it straight away, or wrap in foil when nearly cold and keep for 1–2 days before eating.

Spiced Fig Bars

Makes 24

INGREDIENTS

350g/12oz/2 cups dried figs
3 eggs
175g/6oz/¾ cup granulated sugar
75g/3oz/¾ cup plain flour
5ml/1 tsp baking powder
2.5ml/½ tsp ground cinnamon
1.5ml/¼ tsp ground cloves
1.5ml/¼ tsp grated nutmeg
pinch of salt
75g/3oz/¾ cup walnuts, finely chopped
30ml/2 tbsp brandy or cognac
icing sugar for dusting

1 Preheat the oven to 160°C/325°F/Gas 3. Line a 30 x 20 x 4cm/12 x 8 x 1½in cake tin with greaseproof paper and grease the paper.

2 With a sharp knife, chop the figs roughly. Set aside.

3 In a bowl, whisk the eggs and sugar until well blended. In another bowl, sift together the dry ingredients, then fold into the egg mixture in several batches.

4 Stir the figs, walnuts and brandy or cognac into the bowl until evenly combined.

5 Scrape the mixture into the prepared cake tin and bake for 35–40 minutes until the top is firm and brown. It should still be soft underneath. Leave to cool in the tin for 5 minutes, then unmould and transfer to a sheet of greaseproof paper lightly sprinkled with icing sugar. Cut into bars.

Creamy Lemon Bars

A delicious and luxurious treat, ideal for accompanying a cup of coffee.

Makes 36

INGREDIENTS

50g/2oz/½ cup icing sugar
175g/6oz/1½ cups plain flour
pinch of salt
175g/6oz/¾ cup butter, chopped
For the topping
4 eggs
350g/12oz/1½ cups granulated sugar
grated rind of 1 lemon
120ml/4fl oz/½ cup fresh lemon juice
175g/6oz/¾ cup whipping cream
icing sugar for dusting

1 Preheat the oven to 160°C/325°F/Gas 3. Grease a 33 x 23cm/13 x 9in cake tin. Sift the sugar, flour and salt into a bowl. Rub in the butter until the mixture resembles coarse crumbs.

2 Press the mixture into the bottom of the prepared cake tin. Bake for about 20 minutes until golden brown.

3 Meanwhile, to make the topping, whisk together the eggs and sugar until blended. Add the lemon rind and juice and mix well.

4 Lightly whip the cream and fold into the egg mixture. Pour over the warm crust, return to the oven, and bake for about 40 minutes, until set. Cool completely before cutting into bars. Dust with icing sugar.

Chocolate Raspberry Macaroon Bars

Any seedless preserve, such as strawberry or apricot, can be substituted for raspberry.

Makes 16–18 bars

INGREDIENTS

115g/4oz/1/2 cup unsalted butter
50g/2oz/1/2 cup icing sugar
25g/1oz/1/4 cup cocoa powder
pinch of salt
5ml/1 tsp almond essence
150g/5oz/1 1/4 cups plain flour
For the topping
150g/5oz/scant 1/2 cup seedless raspberry preserve
15ml/1 tbsp raspberry-flavour liqueur
175g/6oz/1 cup mini chocolate chips
175g/6oz/1 1/2 cups finely ground almonds
4 egg whites
pinch of salt
200g/7oz/1 firmly packed cup caster sugar
2.5ml/1/2 tsp almond essence
50g/2oz/1/2 cup flaked almonds

1 Preheat the oven to 160°C/325°F/Gas 3. Invert a 23 x 33cm/9 x 13in cake tin. Mould a sheet of foil over the tin and smooth the foil evenly around the corners. Lift off the foil and turn the tin right side up; line with the moulded foil. Lightly grease the foil.

2 In a medium bowl, with an electric mixer, beat together the butter, sugar, cocoa and salt until well blended. Add in the almond essence and the flour and mix until the mixture forms a crumbly dough.

3 Turn the dough into the prepared tin and pat firmly over the bottom to make an even layer. Prick the dough with a fork.

4 Bake for 20 minutes, until just set. Remove from the oven and increase the temperature to 190°C/375°F/Gas 5.

5 To make the topping, in a small bowl, combine the raspberry preserve and raspberry-flavour liqueur. Spread the topping evenly over the chocolate crust, then sprinkle evenly with the chocolate chips.

6 In a food processor fitted with a metal blade, process the almonds, egg whites, salt, sugar and almond essence until well blended and foamy. Gently pour over the jam layer, spreading evenly to the edges of the tin. Sprinkle with flaked almonds.

7 Bake for 20–25 minutes more, until the top is golden and puffed. Transfer to a wire rack to cool in the tin for 20 minutes, until firm.

8 Using the edges of the foil, carefully remove the cake from the tin and cool completely. Peel off the foil and, using a sharp knife, cut into bars.

Lemon Cheese Bars

Makes 24

INGREDIENTS

115g/4oz/1 cup plain flour
50g/2oz/½ cup chopped walnuts
75g/3oz/½ cup soft light brown sugar
75g/3oz/⅓ cup unsalted butter
grated rind and juice of 1 small lemon
225g/8oz/1 cup full-fat cream cheese
50g/2oz/¼ cup granulated sugar
15ml/1 tbsp milk
2.5ml/½ tsp vanilla essence
1 large egg

1 Preheat the oven to 180°C/350°F/ Gas 4. Grease a 23cm/9in square cake tin.

2 Beat together the flour, walnuts, brown sugar and butter. Divide the mixture in half. Press one half of the mixture into the prepared cake tin. Bake for 12–15 minutes, until lightly browned. Remove from the oven.

3 Beat together the lemon rind and juice, the cheese and sugar, then beat in the milk, vanilla essence and egg. Spoon over the partly cooked pastry and crumble the remaining mixture evenly over the top. Bake for a further 25 minutes, until the top is golden. Transfer to a wire rack to cool, then chill. Cut into bars.

Citrus Spice Bars

Makes 50

INGREDIENTS

115g/4oz/¾ cup candied orange peel, chopped
50g/2oz/⅓ cup seedless raisins
75ml/5 tbsp rum
50g/2oz/3 tbsp clear honey
50g/2oz/3 tbsp black treacle
1 egg
115g/4oz/1 cup ground almonds
175g/6oz/1½ cups wholemeal flour
2.5ml/½ tsp baking powder
large pinch bicarbonate of soda
5ml/1 tsp ground cinnamon
2.5ml/½ tsp ground ginger
115g/4oz/1 cup unblanched almonds, chopped
50g/2oz/½ cup sifted icing sugar
45ml/about 3 tbsp orange juice

1 Preheat the oven to 200°C/400°F/ Gas 6. Lightly grease a 33 x 23cm/ 13 x 9in cake tin. Place the orange peel, raisins and rum in a bowl, cover and set aside for 1 hour.

2 Pour the honey and black treacle into a saucepan and bring to the boil. Set aside to cool, then beat in the egg. Mix together the ground almonds, flour, baking powder, bicarbonate of soda and spices and stir into the mixture. Stir in the chopped almonds and the rum mixture and form into a dough.

3 Press the dough into the prepared cake tin. Bake for about 20 minutes. Transfer to a wire rack to cool. Sift the icing sugar into a bowl and stir in just enough orange juice to make a spreading consistency. Set aside for 1 hour.

4 Spread the icing over the cake. Decorate if you wish and cut into generous bars.

Chocolate and Coconut Slices

Very simple to make, these slices are deliciously moist and sweet.

Makes 24

INGREDIENTS

115g/4oz/½ cup butter or margarine, chopped
175g/6oz digestive biscuits, crushed
50g/2oz/4 tbsp caster sugar
pinch of salt
75g/3oz/1 cup desiccated coconut
250g/9oz/1½ cups plain chocolate chips
250ml/8fl oz/1 cup sweetened condensed milk
115g/4oz/1 cup chopped walnuts

1 Preheat the oven to 180°C/350°F/Gas 4. Melt the butter or margarine in a small saucepan over a low heat.

2 In a bowl, combine the crushed biscuits, sugar, salt and melted butter or margarine. Press the mixture evenly over the bottom of an ungreased 33 x 23cm/13 x 9in baking dish.

3 Sprinkle the coconut over the cookie base, then scatter over the chocolate chips. Pour the condensed milk evenly over the chocolate. Sprinkle the walnuts on top.

4 Bake for 30 minutes. Transfer to a wire rack and leave to cool, preferably overnight. When cooled, cut into slices.

Hermits

Makes 30

INGREDIENTS

75g/3oz/¾ cup plain flour
7.5ml/1½ tsp baking powder
5ml/1 tsp ground cinnamon
2.5ml/½ tsp grated nutmeg
1.5ml/¼ tsp ground cloves
1.5ml/¼ tsp ground allspice
250g/9oz/1½ cups raisins
115g/4oz/½ cup butter or margarine
115g/4oz/½ cup caster sugar
2 eggs
175g/6oz/½ cup black treacle
50g/2oz/½ cup walnuts, chopped

1 Preheat the oven to 180°C/350°F/Gas 4. Line the bottom and sides of a 33 x 23cm/13 x 9in tin with greaseproof paper and grease.

2 Sift together the flour, baking powder and spices into a bowl.

3 Place the raisins in another bowl and toss with a few tablespoons of the flour mixture.

4 With an electric mixer, cream together the butter or margarine and sugar, until light and fluffy. Beat in the eggs, one at a time, then the black treacle. Stir in the flour mixture, raisins and walnuts.

5 Spread evenly in the prepared cake tin. Bake for 15–18 minutes, until just set. Leave to cool in the tin before cutting into squares or fingers.

Butterscotch Meringue Bars

Makes 12

INGREDIENTS

50g/2oz/4 tbsp butter
175g/6oz/1 firmly packed cup dark brown sugar
1 egg
2.5ml/½ tsp vanilla essence
50g/2oz/½ cup plain flour
pinch of salt
1.5ml/¼ tsp grated nutmeg
For the topping
1 egg white
pinch of salt
15ml/1 tbsp golden syrup
115g/4oz/½ cup granulated sugar
50g/2oz/½ cup walnuts, finely chopped

1 Combine the butter and brown sugar in a saucepan and cook until bubbling. Set aside to cool.

2 Preheat the oven to 180°C/350°F/Gas 4. Line a 20cm/8in square cake tin with greaseproof paper and grease the paper.

3 Beat the egg and vanilla essence into the cooled sugar mixture. Sift over the flour, salt and nutmeg and fold in. Spread over the bottom of the prepared cake tin.

4 To make the topping, beat the egg white with the salt until it holds soft peaks. Beat in the golden syrup, then the sugar and continue beating until the mixture holds stiff peaks.

5 Fold in the nuts and spread on top of the mixture in the tin. Bake for 30 minutes. Cut into bars when cool.

Muffins and Scones

Muffins are very easy to make and delicious to eat: to mix the batter, simply use a few swift strokes to stir the liquid ingredients, taking no more than 10–20 seconds. This will leave some lumps. Ignore them. If the batter is mixed for too long, the dough will be toughened and the muffins will be coarse-textured and full of tunnels. Rather than being mixed to a smooth, pouring consistency, the mixture should come off the spoon in coarse dollops.

Muffins are best eaten when freshly made and still warm, certainly on the day of baking. To re-warm muffins, wrap them loosely in foil and heat for approximately 5 minutes in an oven preheated to 230°C/450°F/Gas 8.

The well-risen, oven-baked scones that are now thought to be an essential part of a British afternoon tea, eaten while warm, split, spread with butter and served with cream (preferably clotted) and jam, did not exist before the introduction of raising agents and reliable ovens in Victorian times. The fore-runners of these modern scones were drop scones and griddle cakes, cooked on the stove top.

The secrets of perfect, light, tender scones are not making the dough too wet, handling it quickly and very lightly, and rolling it out with even pressure to the correct thickness – at least 2cm/¾in, and lastly, preheating the oven to quite a high temperature, usually about 220°C/425°F/Gas 7.

Oatmeal Buttermilk Muffins

Makes 12

INGREDIENTS

115g/4oz/1 cup rolled oats
250ml/8fl oz/1 cup buttermilk
115g/4oz/½ cup butter
75g/3oz/½ cup dark brown sugar
1 egg
115g/4oz/1 cup plain flour
5ml/1 tsp baking powder
2.5ml/½ tsp bicarbonate of soda
pinch of salt
25g/1oz/¼ cup raisins

Cook's Tip If buttermilk is not available, add 5ml/1 tsp lemon juice or vinegar to 250ml/8fl oz/1 cup of milk. Let the mixture stand a few minutes to curdle before adding it to the oats.

1 In a bowl, combine the oats and buttermilk and leave to soak for 1 hour.

2 Grease 12 muffin tins, or use paper liners. Preheat the oven to 200°C/400°F/ Gas 6.

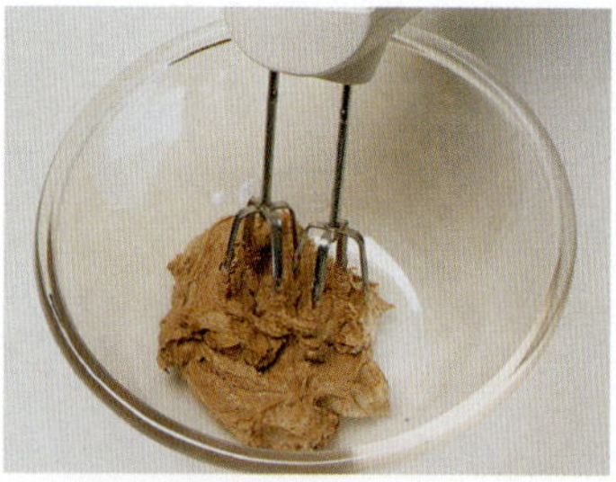

3 With an electric mixer, cream the butter and sugar until light and fluffy. Beat in the egg.

4 Sift together the flour, baking powder, bicarbonate of soda and salt. Stir into the butter mixture, alternating with the oat mixture. Fold in the raisins.

5 Fill the muffin tins two-thirds full. Bake for 20–25 minutes. Transfer to a wire rack to cool.

Pumpkin Muffins

Makes 14

INGREDIENTS

115g/4oz/½ cup butter or margarine
175g/6oz/¾ cup firmly packed brown sugar
115g/4oz/⅓ cup black treacle
1 egg, beaten
225g/8oz/1 cup cooked or canned pumpkin
200g/7oz/1¾ cups plain flour
pinch of salt
5ml/1 tsp bicarbonate of soda
7.5ml/1½ tsp ground cinnamon
5ml/1 tsp grated nutmeg
50g/2oz/¼ cup currants or raisins

1 Preheat the oven to 200°C/400°F/ Gas 6. Grease 14 muffin tins, or use paper liners.

2 With an electric mixer, cream the butter or margarine until soft. Add the sugar and black treacle and beat until light and fluffy.

3 Add the egg and pumpkin and stir until well blended.

4 Sift over the flour, salt, bicarbonate of soda, cinnamon and nutmeg. Fold in until just blended, do not overmix.

5 Fold the currants or raisins into the pumpkin mixture until just evenly combined.

6 Spoon the batter into the prepared muffin tins, filling them two-thirds full.

7 Bake for 12–15 minutes, until the tops spring back when touched lightly. Serve warm or cold.

Banana Muffins

Makes 12

INGREDIENTS

225g/8oz/2 cups plain flour
5ml/1 tsp baking powder
5ml/1 tsp bicarbonate of soda
pinch of salt
2.5ml/½ tsp ground cinnamon
1.5ml/¼ tsp grated nutmeg
3 large ripe bananas
1 egg
50g/2oz/⅓ cup dark brown sugar
50ml/2fl oz/¼ cup vegetable oil
40g/1½oz/¼ cup raisins

1 Preheat the oven to 190°C/375°F/Gas 5.

2 Grease 12 muffin tins, or use paper liners.

3 Sift together the flour, baking powder, bicarbonate of soda, salt, cinnamon and nutmeg. Set aside.

4 With an electric mixer, mash the peeled bananas at moderate speed.

5 Beat the egg, sugar and oil into the mashed bananas.

6 Add the dry ingredients and beat in gradually, on low speed. Mix until just blended. With a wooden spoon, stir in the raisins. Fill the muffin tins two-thirds full.

7 Bake for 20–25 minutes, until the tops spring back when touched lightly. Transfer to a wire rack to cool.

Maple Pecan Muffins

Makes 20

INGREDIENTS

150g/5oz/1¼ cups pecans
300g/11oz/2½ cups plain flour
5ml/1 tsp baking powder
5ml/1 tsp bicarbonate of soda
pinch of salt
1.5ml/¼ tsp ground cinnamon
115g/4oz/½ cup granulated sugar
50g/2oz/⅓ firmly packed cup light brown sugar
45ml/3 tbsp maple syrup
150g/5oz/⅔ cup butter
3 eggs
300ml/½ pint/1¼ cups buttermilk
60 pecan halves to decorate

Variation For Pecan Spice Muffins, substitute an equal quantity of black treacle for the maple syrup. Increase the cinnamon to 2.5ml/½ tsp, and add 5ml/1 tsp ground ginger and 2.5ml/½ tsp grated nutmeg, sifted with the flour and other dry ingredients.

1 Preheat the oven to 180°C/350°F/Gas 4. Grease 20 muffin tins, or use paper liners.

2 Spread the pecans on a baking sheet and toast in the oven for 5 minutes. Leave to cool, then chop coarsely and set aside.

3 In a bowl, sift together the flour, baking powder, bicarbonate of soda, salt and cinnamon. Set aside.

4 In a large mixing bowl, combine the granulated sugar, light brown sugar, maple syrup and butter. Beat with an electric mixer until light and fluffy.

5 Add the eggs, one at a time, beating to incorporate thoroughly after each addition.

6 Pour half of the buttermilk and half of the dry ingredients into the butter mixture, then stir until blended. Repeat with the remaining buttermilk and dry ingredients.

7 Fold the chopped pecans into the batter. Fill the muffin tins two-thirds full. Top with the pecan halves.

8 Bake for 20–25 minutes, until puffed up and golden. Leave to stand for 5 minutes before transferring to a wire rack to cool.

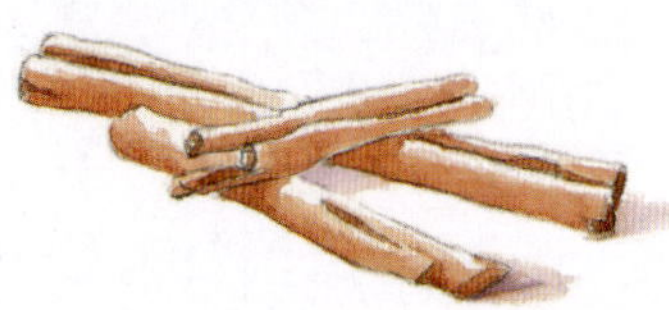

Raspberry Muffins

Low-fat buttermilk gives these muffins a light and spongy texture. They are delicious to eat at any time of day.

Makes 10–12

INGREDIENTS

300g/11oz/2½ cups plain flour
15ml/1 tbsp baking powder
115g/4oz/½ cup caster sugar
1 egg
250ml/8fl oz/1 cup buttermilk
60ml/4 tbsp sunflower oil
150g/5oz/1 cup raspberries

Variation Cranberry Muffins: a tea or breakfast treat that is not too sweet.

350g/12oz/3 cups plain flour
15ml/1 tsp baking powder
pinch of salt
115g/4oz/½ cup caster sugar
2 eggs
150ml/¼ pint/⅔ cup milk
50ml/2fl oz/4 tbsp corn oil
finely grated rind of 1 orange
150g/5oz/1 cup cranberries

1 Preheat the oven to 190°C/375°F/ Gas 5. Line 12 deep muffin tins with paper cases. Mix the flour, baking powder, salt and caster sugar together. Lightly beat the eggs with the milk and oil.

2 Add the liquids to the dry ingredients and blend to make a smooth batter. Divide the mixture between the muffin cases and bake for 25 minutes, until risen and golden. Leave to cool in the tins for a few minutes, and serve warm or cold.

1 Preheat the oven to 200°C/400°F/ Gas 6. Arrange 12 paper cases in deep muffin tins. Sift the flour and baking powder into a mixing bowl, stir in the sugar, then make a well in the centre.

2 Mix the egg, buttermilk and sunflower oil together in a bowl, pour into the flour mixture and mix quickly until just combined.

3 Add the raspberries and lightly fold in with a metal spoon. Spoon the mixture into the paper cases.

4 Bake for 20–25 minutes, until golden brown and firm in the centre. Transfer to a wire rack and serve warm or cold.

Double Chocolate Chip Muffins

These marvellous muffins are packed with chunky plain and white chocolate chips.

Makes 16

INGREDIENTS

400g/14oz/3½ cups plain flour
15ml/1 tbsp baking powder
30ml/2 tbsp cocoa powder
115g/4oz/½ cup dark muscovado sugar
2 eggs
150ml/¼ pint/⅔ cup soured cream
150ml/¼ pint/⅔ cup milk
60ml/4 tbsp sunflower oil
175g/6oz white chocolate
175g/6oz plain chocolate
cocoa powder for dusting

Cook's Tip If soured cream is not available, sour 150ml/¼ pint/⅔ cup single cream by stirring in 5ml/1 tsp lemon juice and letting the mixture stand until thickened.

1 Preheat the oven to 190°C/375°F/ Gas 5. Place 16 paper muffin cases in muffin tins or deep patty tins. Sift the flour, baking powder and cocoa into a bowl and stir in the sugar. Make a well in the centre.

2 In a separate bowl, beat the eggs with the soured cream, milk and oil, then stir into the well in the dry ingredients. Beat well, gradually incorporating the flour mixture to make a thick and creamy batter.

Variation Make sure you use good quality chocolate with a high cocoa content, Vary the proportions of plain and white chocolate, or add in milk chocolate if you prefer.

3 Finely chop the chocolate and stir into the batter mixture.

4 Spoon the mixture into the muffin cases, filling them almost to the top. Bake for 25–30 minutes, until well risen and firm to the touch. Transfer to a wire rack to cool, then dust with cocoa powder.

Chocolate Walnut Muffins

Walnuts and chocolate are a delicious combination.

Makes 12

INGREDIENTS

175g/6oz/¾ cup unsalted butter, chopped
150g/5oz plain chocolate, chopped
225g/8oz/1 cup granulated sugar
50g/2oz/¼ firmly packed cup dark brown sugar
4 eggs
5ml/1 tsp vanilla essence
1.5ml/¼ tsp almond essence
75g/3oz/¾ cup plain flour
115g/4oz/1 cup walnuts, chopped

1 Preheat the oven to 180°C/350°F/ Gas 4. Grease muffin tins, or use paper liners.

2 Melt the butter with the chocolate in the top of a double boiler or a heatproof bowl over a saucepan of hot water. Transfer to a large mixing bowl.

3 Stir both the sugars into the chocolate mixture. Mix in the eggs, one at a time, then add the vanilla and almond essences.

4 Sift over the flour and fold in until evenly combined.

5 Stir the walnuts evenly into the chocolate mixture.

6 Fill the muffin tins almost to the top and bake for 30–35 minutes. Leave to stand for 5 minutes before transferring to a wire rack.

Chocolate Chip Muffins

Use the best quality chocolate chips you can find.

Makes 10

INGREDIENTS

115g/4oz/½ cup butter or margarine
75g/3oz/⅓ cup granulated sugar
30ml/2 tbsp dark brown sugar
2 eggs
175g/6oz/1½ cups plain flour
5ml/1 tsp baking powder
120ml/4fl oz/½ cup milk
175g/6oz/1 cup plain chocolate chips

1 Preheat the oven to 190°C/375°F/ Gas 5. Grease 10 muffin tins, or use paper liners.

2 With an electric mixer, cream the butter or margarine until soft. Add both sugars and beat until light and fluffy. Beat in the eggs, one at a time.

3 Sift the flour and baking powder, twice. Fold into the butter mixture, alternating with the milk.

4 Divide half of the mixture between the muffin tins. Sprinkle several chocolate chips on top, then cover with a spoonful of batter.

5 Bake for about 25 minutes, until lightly coloured. Leave to stand for 5 minutes before transferring to a wire rack to cool.

Banana and Nut Buns

Use walnut pieces instead of pecans if you prefer.

Makes 8

INGREDIENTS

150g/5oz/1¼ cup plain flour
7.5ml/1½ tsp baking powder
50g/2oz/¼ cup butter or margarine
175g/6oz/¾ cup caster sugar
1 egg
1 tsp vanilla essence
3 medium bananas, mashed
50g/2oz/½ cup chopped pecans
75ml/3 fl oz/⅓ cup milk

1 Preheat the oven to 190°C/375°F/Gas 5. Grease eight patty tins.

2 Sift the flour and baking powder into a small bowl. Set aside.

3 With an electric mixer, cream together the butter or margarine and the sugar. Add the egg and vanilla essence and beat until fluffy. Mix in the bananas.

4 Add the pecans. With the mixer on low speed, beat in the flour mixture alternately with the milk. Spoon the mixture into the prepared tins. Bake for 20–25 minutes, until a skewer or cake tester inserted in the centre of a bun comes out clean.

5 Leave to cool in the patty tins for 10 minutes. Unmould on to the wire rack. Cool for 10 minutes longer before serving.

Fruit and Cinnamon Buns

Makes 8

INGREDIENTS

115g/4oz/1 cup plain flour
15ml/1 tbsp baking powder
pinch of salt
65g/2½oz/scant ½ cup light brown sugar
1 egg
175ml/6fl oz/¾ cup milk
45ml/3 tbsp vegetable oil
10ml/2 tsp ground cinnamon
150g/5oz/1 cup fresh or thawed frozen blueberries, or blackcurrants

1 Preheat the oven to 190°C/375°F/Gas 5. Grease eight patty tins.

2 With an electric mixer, beat together the first eight ingredients until smooth.

3 Fold the blueberries or blackcurrants into the other ingredients until just evenly combined.

4 Spoon the mixture into the patty tins, filling them two-thirds full. Bake for about 25 minutes, until a skewer or cake tester inserted in the centre of a bun comes out clean.

5 Leave to cool in the patty tins, on a wire rack, for 10 minutes, then transfer the buns to the wire rack and leave to cool completely.

Carrot Muffins

Makes 12

INGREDIENTS

175g/6oz/3/4 cup margarine
75g/3oz/1/2 cup dark brown sugar
1 egg
15ml/1 tbsp water
275g/10oz/2 cups grated carrots
150g/5oz/1 1/4 cups plain flour
5ml/1 tsp baking powder
2.5ml/1/2 tsp bicarbonate of soda
5ml/1 tsp ground cinnamon
1.5ml/1/4 tsp grated nutmeg
pinch of salt

1 Preheat the oven to 180°C/350°F/Gas 4. Grease 12 muffin tins, or use paper liners.

2 With an electric mixer, cream the margarine and sugar until light and fluffy. Beat in the egg and water.

3 Stir the grated carrots into the creamed mixture until evenly combined. Sift over the flour, baking powder, bicarbonate of soda, cinnamon, nutmeg and salt. Stir to blend evenly.

4 Spoon the batter into the prepared muffin tins, filling them almost to the top.

5 Bake for about 35 minutes, until the tops spring back when touched lightly. Leave to stand for 10 minutes before transferring to a wire rack to cool.

Dried Cherry Muffins

If you can't find dried cherries, use the same amount of dried cranberries.

Makes 16

INGREDIENTS

250ml/8fl oz/1 cup plain yogurt
225g/8oz/1 cup dried cherries
115g/4oz/1/2 cup butter
175g/6oz/3/4 cup caster sugar
2 eggs
5ml/1 tsp vanilla essence
200g/7oz/1 3/4 cups plain flour
10ml/2 tsp baking powder
5ml/1 tsp bicarbonate of soda
pinch of salt

1 In a mixing bowl, combine the yogurt and cherries. Cover and leave to stand for 30 minutes.

2 Preheat the oven to 180°C/350°F/Gas 4. Grease 16 muffin tins, or use paper liners.

3 With an electric mixer, cream together the butter and sugar until light and fluffy.

4 Add the eggs, one at a time, beating well after each addition. Add the vanilla essence and the cherry mixture and stir to blend. Set aside.

5 In another bowl, sift together the flour, baking powder, bicarbonate of soda and salt. Fold into the cherry mixture in three batches; do not overmix.

6 Fill the prepared muffin tins two-thirds full. Bake for about 20 minutes until the tops spring back when touched lightly. Transfer to a wire rack to cool.

Blueberry Muffins

Makes 12

INGREDIENTS

175g/6oz/1¼ cups plain flour
75g/3oz/⅓ cup caster sugar
10ml/2 tsp baking powder
pinch of salt
2 eggs
50g/2oz/4 tbsp butter, melted
175ml/6fl oz/¾ cup milk
5ml/1 tsp vanilla essence
5ml/1 tsp grated lemon rind
150g/5oz/1 cup fresh blueberries

1 Preheat the oven to 200°C/400°F/Gas 6. Grease 12 muffin tins, or use paper liners.

2 Sift the flour, sugar, baking powder and salt into a bowl. Whisk the eggs until blended. Stir in the melted butter, milk, vanilla essence and lemon rind.

3 Make a well in the dry ingredients and pour in the egg mixture. With a large metal spoon, stir until the flour is just moistened, not until smooth.

4 Rinse the blueberries and dry well, then gently fold into the batter with a metal spoon, making sure they are distributed evenly.

5 Spoon the batter into the tins, leaving room for the muffins to rise. Bake for 20–25 minutes. Leave to cool for 5 minutes before transferring to a wire rack to cool.

Date and Apple Muffins

These muffins are delicious and very filling.

Makes 12

INGREDIENTS

150g/5oz/1 1/4 cups self-raising wholemeal flour
150g/5oz/1 1/4 cups self-raising white flour
5ml/1 tsp ground cinnamon
5ml/1 tsp baking powder
25g/1oz/2 tbsp margarine
75g/3oz/1/2 cup light muscovado sugar
1 eating apple
250ml/8fl oz/1 cup apple juice
30ml/2 tbsp pear and apple spread
1 egg, lightly beaten
75g/3oz/1/2 cup chopped dates
15ml/1 tbsp chopped pecans

1 Preheat the oven to 200°C/400°F/Gas 6. Arrange 12 paper cases in a deep muffin tin. Put the wholemeal flour in a mixing bowl. Sift in the white flour with the cinnamon and baking powder. Rub in the margarine until the mixture resembles breadcrumbs, then stir in the muscovado sugar.

2 Quarter and core the apple, chop the flesh finely and set aside. Stir a little of the apple juice with the pear and apple spread until smooth. Mix in the remaining juice, then add to the rubbed-in mixture with the beaten egg.

3 Add the chopped apple to the bowl with the dates. Mix quickly until just combined. Divide the mixture among the muffin cases.

4 Sprinkle with the chopped pecans. Bake the muffins for 20–25 minutes, until golden brown and firm in the middle. Transfer to a wire rack and serve while still warm.

Blackberry Muffins

Other berries, such as elderberries or blueberries, can be substituted for the blackberries.

Makes 12

INGREDIENTS

275g/10oz/2½ cups plain white flour
50g/2oz/generous ¼ cup light brown sugar
20ml/4 tsp baking powder
pinch of salt
65g/2½oz/generous ½ cup chopped blanched almonds
90g/3½oz/generous ½ cup fresh blackberries
2 eggs
200ml/7fl oz/⅞ cup milk
65g/2½oz/4 tbsp butter, melted
15ml/1 tbsp sloe gin
15ml/1 tbsp rosewater

1 Mix the flour, sugar, baking powder and salt in a bowl and stir in the almonds and blackberries, mixing them well to coat with the flour mixture.

2 Preheat the oven to 200°C/400°F/Gas 6. Grease 12 muffin tins, or use paper liners.

3 In another bowl, mix the eggs with the milk, then gradually add the butter, sloe gin and rosewater. Make a well in the centre of the bowl of dry ingredients and add the egg and milk mixture. Stir well. Spoon the mixture into the muffin tins or cases. Bake for 20–25 minutes, until browned. Transfer to a wire rack to cool.

Chocolate Blueberry Muffins

Blueberries are one of the few fruits that combine deliciously with chocolate.

Makes 12

INGREDIENTS

115g/4oz/½ cup butter
75g/3oz plain chocolate, chopped
200g/7oz/generous 1 cup granulated sugar
1 egg, lightly beaten
250ml/8fl oz/1 cup buttermilk
10ml/2 tsp vanilla essence
275g/10oz/2½ cups plain flour
5ml/1 tsp bicarbonate of soda
175g/6oz/generous 1 cup fresh or frozen blueberries, thawed
25g/1oz plain chocolate, melted, to decorate

1 Preheat the oven to 190°C/375°F/Gas 5. Grease 12 deep patty tins, or use paper liners. In a medium saucepan over a medium heat, melt the butter and chocolate until smooth, stirring frequently. Remove from the heat and leave to cool slightly.

2 Stir in the sugar, egg, buttermilk and vanilla essence. Gently fold in the flour and bicarbonate of soda until just blended. (Do not overblend; although the mixture may be lumpy with some unblended flour.) Fold in the berries.

3 Spoon the batter into the prepared bun tins, filling to the top. Bake for 25–30 minutes, until a skewer or cake tester inserted in the centre comes out with just a few crumbs attached. Remove the muffins in their paper liners to a wire rack immediately (if left in the tin they will go soggy). To decorate, drizzle with the melted chocolate and serve warm or cool.

Prune Muffins

Buy the ready-to-eat prunes if you can, as these are already soaked and pitted.

Makes 12

INGREDIENTS

1 egg
250ml/8fl oz/1 cup milk
50ml/2fl oz/¼ cup vegetable oil
50g/2oz/¼ cup granulated sugar
30ml/2 tbsp dark brown sugar
225g/8oz/2 cups plain flour
10ml/2 tsp baking powder
pinch of salt
1.5ml/¼ tsp grated nutmeg
150g/5oz/¾ cup cooked pitted prunes, chopped

1 Preheat the oven to 200°C/400°F/Gas 6. Grease 12 muffin tins or use paper liners.

2 Break the egg into a mixing bowl and beat with a fork. Beat in the milk and oil.

3 Stir the sugars into the egg mixture. Set aside. Sift the flour, baking powder, salt and nutmeg into a mixing bowl. Make a well in the centre, pour in the egg mixture and stir. The batter should be slightly lumpy.

4 Gently fold the prunes into the batter until just evenly distributed. Fill the prepared muffin tins two-thirds full.

5 Bake for about 20 minutes, until golden brown. Leave to stand for 10 minutes before transferring to a wire rack. Serve warm or at room temperature.

Yogurt Honey Muffins

Makes 12

INGREDIENTS

50g/2oz/4 tbsp butter
75g/3oz/5 tbsp clear honey
250ml/8fl oz/1 cup plain yogurt
1 egg
grated rind of 1 lemon
50ml/2fl oz/¼ cup lemon juice
115g/4oz/1 cup plain flour
115g/4oz/1 cup wholemeal flour
7.5ml/1½ tsp bicarbonate of soda
pinch of grated nutmeg

Variation For Walnut Yogurt Honey Muffins, add 50g/2oz/½ cup chopped walnuts, folded in with the flour. This makes a more substantial muffin.

1 Preheat the oven to 190°C/375°F/Gas 5. Grease 12 muffin tins, or use paper liners.

2 In a saucepan, melt the butter and honey. Remove from the heat and set aside to cool slightly.

3 In a bowl, whisk together the yogurt, egg, lemon rind and juice. Add the butter and honey mixture. Set aside.

4 In another bowl, sift together the dry ingredients. Fold the dry ingredients into the yogurt mixture just to blend.

5 Fill the prepared muffin tins two-thirds full. Bake for 20–25 minutes until the tops spring back when touched lightly. Leave to cool in the pan for 5 minutes before transferring to a wire rack. Serve warm or at room temperature.

Raisin Bran Muffins

Makes 15

INGREDIENTS

50g/2oz/4 tbsp butter or margarine
75g/3oz/⅔ cup plain flour
50g/2oz/½ cup wholemeal flour
7.5ml/1½ tsp bicarbonate of soda
pinch of salt
5ml/1 tsp ground cinnamon
25g/1oz/½ cup bran
75g/3oz/½ cup raisins
50g/2oz/⅓ cup dark brown sugar
50g/2oz/¼ cup granulated sugar
1 egg
250ml/8fl oz/1 cup buttermilk
juice of ½ lemon

1 Preheat the oven to 200°C/400°F/Gas 6. Grease 15 muffin tins, or use paper liners.

2 Place the butter or margarine in a saucepan and melt over a low heat. Set aside. In a mixing bowl, sift together the plain flour, wholemeal flour, bicarbonate of soda, salt and cinnamon.

3 Add the bran, raisins, and sugars and stir until blended. In another bowl, mix together the egg, buttermilk, lemon juice and melted butter or margarine.

4 Add the buttermilk mixture to the dry ingredients and stir lightly and quickly until just moistened; do not mix until smooth.

5 Spoon the batter into the prepared muffin tins, filling them almost to the top. Bake for 15–20 minutes, until golden. Serve warm or at room temperature.

Raspberry Crumble Muffins

Makes 12

INGREDIENTS

175g/6oz/1½ cups plain flour
10ml/2 tsp baking powder
pinch of salt
5ml/1 tsp ground cinnamon
50g/2oz/¼ cup granulated sugar
50g/2oz/¼ firmly packed cup light brown sugar
115g/4oz/½ cup butter, melted
1 egg
120ml/4fl oz/½ cup milk
225g/8oz/1¼ cups fresh raspberries
grated rind of 1 lemon
For the crumble topping
50g/2oz/¼ cup pecans, finely chopped
50g/2oz/¼ firmly packed cup dark brown sugar
45ml/3 tbsp plain flour
5ml/1 tsp ground cinnamon
40g/1½oz/3 tbsp butter, melted

1 Preheat the oven to 180°C/350°F/Gas 4. Grease 12 muffin tins, or use paper liners. Sift the flour, baking powder, salt and cinnamon into a bowl. Add the sugars, and stir to blend.

2 Make a well in the centre of the mixture. Place the butter, egg and milk in the well and mix until just combined. Stir in the raspberries and lemon rind. Spoon the batter into the prepared muffin tins, filling them almost to the top.

3 To make the crumble topping, mix the pecans, dark brown sugar, flour and cinnamon in a bowl. Stir in the melted butter.

4 Spoon some of the crumble over each muffin. Bake for about 25 minutes. Transfer to a wire rack to cool slightly. Serve warm.

Nutty Muffins with Walnut Liqueur

Walnut liqueur gives a lift to these deep American muffins.

Makes 12–14

INGREDIENTS

225g/8oz/2 cups plain flour
20ml/4 tsp baking powder
2.5ml/½ tsp mixed spice
pinch of salt
115g/4oz/⅔ cup soft light brown sugar
75g/3oz/¾ cup chopped walnuts
50g/2oz/4 tbsp butter, melted
2 eggs
175ml/6fl oz/¾ cup milk
30ml/2 tbsp walnut liqueur
For the topping
30ml/2 tbsp soft dark brown sugar
25g/1oz/¼ cup chopped walnuts

1 Preheat the oven to 200°C/400°F/ Gas 6. Grease 12–14 muffin tins or deep bun tins, or use paper muffin cases supported in muffin tins. Sift the flour, baking powder, mixed spice and salt into a mixing bowl, then stir in the sugar and chopped walnuts.

2 In a jug, combine the melted butter, eggs, milk and liqueur.

3 Pour the butter mixture into the dry mixture and stir for just long enough to combine the ingredients. The batter should be lumpy.

4 Fill the muffin or bun tins two-thirds full, then top with a sprinkling of sugar and walnuts. Bake for 15 minutes until the muffins are golden brown. Leave in the tins for a few minutes, then transfer to a wire rack to cool.

Apple and Cinnamon Muffins

These spicy muffins are quick and easy to make and are perfect for serving for breakfast or tea.

Makes 6

INGREDIENTS

1 egg, beaten
40g/1½oz/3 tbsp caster sugar
120ml/4fl oz/½ cup milk
50g/2 oz/¼ cup butter, melted
150g/5oz/1¼ cups plain flour
7.5ml/1½ tsp baking powder
pinch of salt
2.5ml/½ tsp ground cinnamon
2 small eating apples, peeled, cored and finely chopped
For the topping
12 brown sugar cubes, roughly crushed
5ml/1 tsp ground cinnamon

Cook's Tip Do not overmix the muffin mixture – it should be lumpy.

1 Preheat the oven to 200°C/400°F/ Gas 6. Line six large muffin tins with paper cases. Mix the egg, sugar, milk and melted butter in a large bowl. Sift in the flour, baking powder, salt and cinnamon. Add the chopped apple and mix roughly.

2 Spoon the mixture into the prepared muffin cases. To make the topping, mix the crushed sugar cubes with the cinnamon. Sprinkle over the uncooked muffins.

3 Bake for 30–35 minutes, until well risen and golden. Transfer to a wire rack to cool.

Pineapple and Cinnamon Drop Scones

Making the batter with pineapple juice instead of milk cuts down on fat and adds to the taste.

Makes 24

INGREDIENTS

115g/4oz/1 cup self-raising wholemeal flour
115g/4oz/1 cup self-raising white flour
5ml/1 tsp ground cinnamon
15ml/1 tbsp caster sugar
1 egg
300ml/½ pint/1¼ cups pineapple juice
75g/3oz/½ cup semi-dried pineapple, chopped

Cook's Tip Drop scones do not keep well and are best eaten freshly cooked.

1 Preheat a griddle, heavy-based frying pan or an electric frying pan. Put the wholemeal flour in a mixing bowl. Sift in the white flour, add the cinnamon and sugar and make a well in the centre. Add the egg with half of the pineapple juice.

2 Gradually incorporate the flour to make a smooth batter. Beat in the remaining juice with the chopped pineapple.

3 Lightly grease the griddle or pan. Drop tablespoons of the batter on to the surface, leaving them until they bubble and the bubbles begin to burst.

4 Turn the drop scones with a palette knife and cook until the underside is golden brown. Continue to cook in successive batches.

Chocolate Chip Banana Drop Scones

These delicious moist scones are topped with cream and toasted almonds.

Makes 16

INGREDIENTS

2 ripe bananas
200ml/7fl oz/7/8 cup milk
2 eggs
150g/5oz/1 1/4 cups self-raising flour
25g/1oz/1/4 cup ground almonds
15ml/1 tbsp caster sugar
pinch of salt
25g/1oz/1 1/2 tbsp plain chocolate chips
butter for frying

For the topping
150ml/1/4 pint/2/3 cup double cream
15ml/1 tbsp icing sugar
50g/2oz/1/2 cup toasted flaked almonds, to decorate

Cook's Tip For banana and blueberry pancakes, replace the chocolate with 115g/4oz/1 cup fresh blueberries. Hot drop scones are also delicious when accompanied by ice cream.

1 In a bowl, mash the bananas with a fork, combine with half of the milk and beat in the eggs. Sieve in the flour, ground almonds, sugar and salt. Make a well in the centre and pour in the remaining milk. Add the chocolate chips and stir to produce a thick batter.

2 Heat a knob of butter in a non-stick frying pan. Spoon the pancake mixture into heaps, allowing room for them to spread. When the mixture starts to bubble, turn the pancakes over and cook briefly on the other side.

3 Lightly whip the cream with the icing sugar to sweeten it slightly. Spoon the cream on to the pancakes and decorate with flaked almonds.

Teatime Scones

Makes 16

INGREDIENTS

225g/8oz/2 cups plain flour
pinch of salt
2.5ml/½ tsp bicarbonate of soda
5ml/1 tsp cream of tartar
25g/1oz/2 tbsp butter
about 150ml/¼ pint/⅔ cup milk or buttermilk

Variation These traditional favourites can be varied by adding 15–30ml/1–2 tbsp of chocolate drops or 5–10/1–2 tsp ground cinnamon.

1 Preheat the oven to 220°C/425°F/Gas 7. Flour a baking sheet. Sift the flour, salt, bicarbonate of soda and cream of tartar into a bowl.

2 Rub in the fat until the mixture resembles fine breadcrumbs. Gradually stir in just enough milk to make a light, spongy dough.

3 Turn the dough on to a lightly-floured surface and knead until smooth. Roll to 2.5cm/1in thick. Cut into rounds with a floured 5cm/2in cutter (or a 4cm/1½in cutter for cocktail savouries).

4 Place the scones on the prepared baking sheet and brush the tops with milk. Bake for 7–10 minutes, until the scones are well risen and golden brown.

Lavender Scones

Serve these scented scones warm, with plum jam and clotted cream.

Makes 12

INGREDIENTS

225g/8oz/2 cups flour
15ml/1 tbsp baking powder
50g/2oz/4 tbsp butter
40g/1½oz/¼ cup caster sugar
10ml/2 tsp fresh lavender florets or 5ml/1 tsp dried culinary lavender, roughly chopped
about 175ml/6fl oz/¾ cup milk

1 Preheat the oven to 220°C/425°F/Gas 7. Grease a baking sheet. Sift together the flour and baking powder. Rub the butter into the dry ingredients until the mixture resembles breadcrumbs.

2 Stir in the sugar and lavender florets, reserving a pinch of lavender to sprinkle on the top of the scones before baking them.

3 Add enough milk to make a soft, sticky dough. Bind the mixture together and then turn the dough on to a well-floured work surface.

4 Shape the dough into a circle, and roll out to 2.5cm/1in depth. Using a floured cutter, stamp out 12 scones.

5 Place on the prepared baking sheet. Brush the tops with a little milk and sprinkle with the reserved lavender.

6 Bake for 10–12 minutes, until golden.

Sunflower Sultana Scones

Makes 10–12

INGREDIENTS

225g/8oz/2 cups self-raising flour
5ml/1 tsp baking powder
25g/1oz/2 tbsp margarine
30ml/2 tbsp golden caster sugar
50g/2oz/⅓ cup sultanas
30ml/2 tbsp sunflower seeds
150g/5oz/⅔ cup natural yogurt
about 30–45ml/2–3 tbsp milk

1 Preheat the oven to 230°C/450°F/Gas 8. Lightly oil a baking sheet. Sift the flour and baking powder into a bowl and rub in the margarine. Stir in the sugar, sultanas and half of the sunflower seeds, then mix in the natural yogurt.

2 Add just enough milk to the mixture to make a soft dough.

3 Roll out on a lightly floured surface to about 2cm/¾ in thick. Cut into 6cm/2½ in rounds with a floured biscuit cutter and lift on to the baking sheet.

4 Brush the tops of the scones with milk and sprinkle with the reserved sunflower seeds.

5 Bake for 10–12 minutes, until well risen and golden brown. Transfer to a wire rack. Serve while still warm, with jam, butter or low-fat spread.

Wholemeal Scones

Wholemeal scones are both delicious and healthy.

Makes 16

INGREDIENTS

175g/6oz/3/4 cup cold butter
225g/8oz/2 cups wholemeal flour
115g/4oz/1 cup plain flour
30ml/2 tbsp caster sugar
pinch of salt
12.5ml/2 1/2 tsp baking soda
2 eggs
175ml/6fl oz/3/4 cup buttermilk
40g/1 1/2oz/1/4 cup raisins

1 Preheat the oven to 200°C/400°F/Gas 6. Grease and flour a large baking sheet.

2 Cut the butter into small pieces. Combine the dry ingredients in a bowl. Add the butter and rub in until the mixture resembles coarse crumbs. Set aside.

3 In another bowl, whisk together the eggs and buttermilk. Set aside 30ml/2 tbsp for glazing.

4 Stir the remaining egg mixture into the dry ingredients until it just holds together. Stir in the raisins.

5 Roll out the dough about 2cm/3/4in thick. Stamp out circles with a floured cookie cutter. Place on the prepared baking sheet and brush with the glaze.

6 Bake for 12–15 minutes until golden. Allow to cool slightly before serving. Split in half with a fork while still warm and spread with butter and jam, if wished.

Orange Raisin Scones

Makes 16

INGREDIENTS

225g/8oz/2 cups plain flour
25ml/1 1/2 tbsp baking powder
75g/3oz/1/3 cup caster sugar
pinch of salt
65g/2 1/2oz/5 tbsp butter, chopped
grated rind of 1 large orange
50g/2oz/1/3 cup raisins
115g/4oz/1/2 cup buttermilk
milk for glazing

1 Preheat the oven to 220°C/425°F/Gas 7. Grease and flour a large baking sheet.

2 Combine the dry ingredients in a large bowl. Add the butter and rub in until the mixture resembles coarse crumbs.

3 Add the orange rind and raisins. Gradually stir in the buttermilk to form a soft dough.

4 Roll out the dough on a floured surface to about 2cm/3/4in thick. Stamp out circles with a floured cookie cutter.

5 Place on the prepared baking sheet and brush the tops with milk. Bake for 12–15 minutes until golden. Serve hot or warm, with butter or whipped cream, and jam.

Cook's Tip For light, delicate scones, handle the dough as little as possible. If you wish, split the scones when cool and toast them under a preheated grill. Butter them while they are still hot.

Cookies for Kids

This chapter includes recipes that are suitable for children to eat, like Gingerbread Teddies, and recipes that children can make themselves. Quite a number of cookie recipes do not even need to be baked, such as Date Crunch, Fruit and Nut Clusters and Marshmallow Crispie Cakes.

Kids – before you embark on a cookie-making session, there are a few guidelines that will help you towards ending up with a batch to be proud of. Start by washing and drying your hands. If your hair is long, tie it back. Wear an apron both to protect your clothes from the food, and to protect the food from your clothes. Make sure the kitchen surfaces are clean and tidy before you begin.

Next, read through the recipe from start to finish very carefully so you can make sure you have all the ingredients and equipment you will need, and so you have a clear idea of what you are going to be doing and in what order. Now you can get out all the equipment you'll need, and assemble and carefully weigh all the ingredients.

Follow the recipe exactly and take your time. Avoid any distractions or interruptions, such as friends or brothers or sisters coming in, or the radio playing, in case you make a mistake or forget where you are in the recipe. If you are in any doubt about anything at all, at any time, or feel you need a hand, don't hesitate to ask a grown-up.

Chewy Fruit Muesli Slice

An easy recipe which needs just weighing out, mixing and baking.

Makes 8

INGREDIENTS

75g/3oz/½ cup ready-to-eat dried apricots, chopped
1 eating apple, cored and grated
150g/5oz/1¼ cups Swiss-style muesli
150ml/¼ pint/⅔ cup apple juice
15g/½oz/1 tbsp soft sunflower margarine

1 Preheat the oven to 190°C/375°F/ Gas 5. Place all the ingredients in a large bowl and mix well.

2 Press the mixture into a 20cm/8in non-stick sandwich tin and bake for 35–40 minutes, until lightly browned and firm.

3 Mark the muesli slice into eight wedges and leave to cool in the tin.

Oat and Apricot Clusters

Here is a variation on an old favourite which children can easily make themselves, so have plenty of the dried fruits and nuts ready for them to add.

Makes 12

INGREDIENTS

50g/2oz/4 tbsp butter or margarine
50g/2oz/3 tbsp clear honey
50g/2oz/$^1/_2$ cup medium oatmeal
50g/2oz/$^1/_3$ cup chopped ready-to-eat dried apricots
15ml/1 tbsp dried banana chips
15ml/1 tbsp dried shreds of coconut
50–75g/2–3oz/2–3 cups cornflakes or Rice Crispies

1 Place the butter or margarine and honey in a small saucepan and warm over a low heat, stirring.

2 Add the oatmeal, apricots, banana chips, coconut and cornflakes or Rice Crispies and mix well.

3 Spoon the mixture into 12 paper cake cases, piling it up roughly. Transfer to a baking sheet, or a tray, and chill until set and firm.

Cook's Tip The ingredients can be changed according to what's in your store cupboard – try peanuts, pecans, raisins or dates.

Fruit and Nut Clusters

This is a fun no-cook recipe which children will like.

Makes 24

INGREDIENTS

225g/8oz white chocolate
50g/2oz/⅓ cup sunflower seeds
50g/2oz/½ cup almond slivers
50g/2oz/⅓ cup sesame seeds
50g/2oz/⅓ cup seedless raisins
5ml/1 tsp ground cinnamon

1 Break the white chocolate into small pieces. Put the chocolate into a heatproof bowl over a saucepan of hot water on a low heat. Do not allow the water to touch the base of the bowl, or the chocolate may become too hot.

2 Alternatively, put the chocolate in a microwave-proof container and heat it on Medium for 3 minutes. Stir the melted chocolate until it is smooth and glossy.

3 Mix the remaining ingredients together, pour on the chocolate and stir well.

4 Using a teaspoon, spoon the mixture into paper cases and leave to set.

Marshmallow Crispie Cakes

Makes 45

INGREDIENTS

250g/9oz bag of toffees
50g/2oz/4 tbsp butter
45ml/3 tbsp milk
115g/4oz/1 cup marshmallows
175g/6oz/6 cups Rice Crispies

1 Lightly brush a 20 x 33cm/8 x 13in roasting tin with a little oil. Put the toffees, butter and milk in a saucepan and heat gently, stirring until the toffees have melted.

2 Add the marshmallows and cereal and stir until well mixed and the marshmallows have melted.

3 Spoon the mixture into the prepared roasting tin, level the surface and leave to set.

4 When cool and hard, cut into squares, remove from the tin, and put into paper cases to serve.

Date Crunch

Makes 24

INGREDIENTS

225g/8oz packet sweetmeal biscuits
75g/3oz/⅓ cup butter
30ml/2 tbsp golden syrup
75g/3oz/½ cup stoned dates, finely chopped
75g/3oz sultanas
150g/5oz milk or plain chocolate, chopped

Cook's Tip For an alternative topping, drizzle 75g/3oz melted white and 75g/3oz melted dark chocolate over.

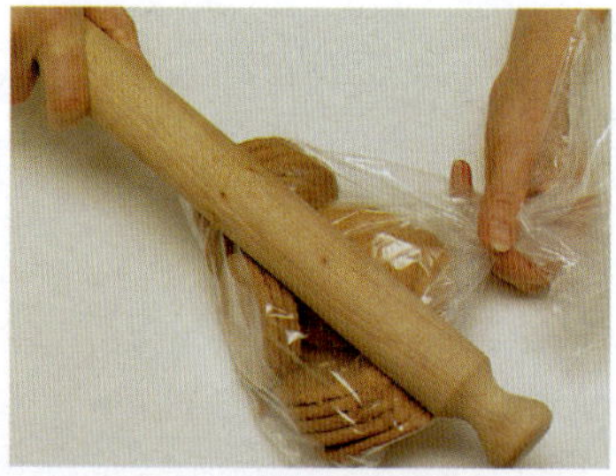

1 Line an 18cm/7in square shallow cake tin with foil. Put the biscuits in a plastic bag and crush roughly with a rolling pin.

2 Gently heat the butter and syrup in a small saucepan until the butter has melted.

3 Stir in the crushed biscuits, the dates and sultanas and mix well. Spoon into the prepared tin, press flat with the back of a spoon and chill for 1 hour.

4 Melt the chocolate in a heatproof bowl, over a saucepan of hot water, stirring until smooth. Spoon over the cookie mixture, spreading evenly with a palette knife. Chill until set. Lift the foil out of the cake tin and peel away. Cut the crunch into 24 pieces and arrange on a plate.

Peanut Cookies

Packing up a picnic? Got a birthday party coming up? Make sure some of these nutty cookies are on the menu.

Makes 25

INGREDIENTS

225g/8oz/1 cup butter
30ml/2 tbsp smooth peanut butter
115g/4oz/1 cup icing sugar
50g/2oz/½ cup cornflour
225g/8oz/2 cups plain flour
115g/4oz/1 cup unsalted peanuts

1 Put the butter and peanut butter in a bowl and beat together. Add the icing sugar, cornflour and plain flour and mix together to make a soft dough.

2 Preheat the oven to 180°C/350°F/Gas 4. Lightly oil two baking sheets. Roll the mixture into 25 small balls, using your hands and place on the baking sheets. Leave plenty of room for the cookies to spread.

3 Press the tops of the balls of dough flat, using either the back of a fork or your fingertips.

4 Press a few of the peanuts into each of the cookies. Bake for 15–20 minutes, until lightly browned. Leave to cool for a few minutes before lifting them carefully on to a wire rack with a palette knife.

Cook's Tip Make really monster cookies by rolling bigger balls of dough. Remember to leave plenty of room on the baking sheets for them to spread, though.

Chocolate Crackle-tops

Older children will enjoy making these distinctive cookies.

Makes 38

INGREDIENTS

200g/7oz plain chocolate, chopped
90g/3½oz/scant ½ cup unsalted butter
115g/4oz/½ cup caster sugar
3 eggs
5ml/1 tsp vanilla essence
215g/7½oz/scant 2 cups plain flour
25g/1oz/¼ cup unsweetened cocoa
2.5ml/½ tsp baking powder
pinch of salt
175g/6oz/1½ cups icing sugar for coating

1 In a medium saucepan over a low heat, melt the chocolate and butter together until smooth, stirring frequently.

2 Remove from the heat. Stir in the sugar, and continue stirring for 2–3 minutes, until the sugar dissolves. Add the eggs one at a time, beating well after each addition; stir in the vanilla.

3 Into a bowl, sift together the flour, cocoa, baking powder and salt. Gradually stir into the chocolate mixture in batches, until just blended.

4 Cover the dough and refrigerate for at least 1 hour, until the dough is cold and holds its shape.

5 Preheat the oven to 160°C/325°F/Gas 3. Grease two or more large baking sheets. Place the icing sugar in a small, deep bowl. Using a small ice-cream scoop or round teaspoon, scoop cold dough into small balls and, between the palms of your hands, roll into 4cm/1½in balls.

6 Drop each ball into the icing sugar and roll until heavily coated. Remove with a slotted spoon and tap against the side of the bowl to remove excess sugar. Place on the prepared baking sheets 4cm/1½in apart.

7 Bake the cookies for 10–15 minutes, until the tops feel slightly firm when touched. Remove the baking sheet to a wire rack for 2–3 minutes. With a metal palette knife, remove the cookies to a wire rack to cool completely.

Chocolate Dominoes

A recipe for children to eat rather than make. Ideal for birthday parties.

Makes 16

INGREDIENTS

175g/6oz/¾ cup soft margarine
175g/6oz/¾ cup caster sugar
150g/5oz/1¼ cups self-raising flour
25g/1oz/¼ cup cocoa powder, sifted
3 eggs
For the topping
175g/6oz/¾ cup butter
25g/1oz/¼ cup cocoa powder
300g/11oz/2½ cups icing sugar
a few liquorice strips and 115g/4oz packet M & M's, for decoration

Variation To make Traffic Light Cakes, omit the cocoa and add an extra 25g/1oz/3 tbsp plain flour. Omit cocoa from the icing and add an extra 25g/1oz/4 tbsp icing sugar and 2.5ml/½ tsp vanilla essence. Spread over the cakes and decorate with red, yellow and green glacé cherries to look like traffic lights.

1 Preheat the oven to 180°C/350°F/ Gas 4. Lightly brush an 18 x 28cm/7 x 11in baking tin with a little oil and line the base of the tin with greaseproof paper.

2 Put all the cake ingredients in a bowl and beat until smooth.

3 Spoon into the prepared cake tin and level the surface with a palette knife.

4 Bake for 30 minutes, until the cake springs back when pressed with the fingertips.

5 Cool in the tin for 5 minutes, then loosen the edges with a knife and transfer to a wire rack. Peel off the paper and leave the cake to cool. Turn the cake on to a chopping board and cut into 16 bars.

6 To make the topping, place the butter in a bowl, sift in the cocoa and icing sugar and beat until smooth. Spread the topping evenly over the cakes with a palette knife.

7 Add a strip of liquorice to each cake, decorate with M & M's for domino dots and arrange the cakes on a serving plate.

Lemony Peanut Pairs

For those who don't like peanut butter, use buttercream or chocolate-and-nut spread instead.

Makes 8–10

INGREDIENTS

40g/1½oz/¼ cup soft light brown sugar
50g/2oz/¼ cup soft margarine
5ml/1 tsp grated lemon rind
75g/3oz/¾ cup wholemeal flour
50g/2oz/¼ cup chopped crystallized pineapple
25g/1oz/2 tbsp smooth peanut butter
sifted icing sugar for dusting

1 Preheat the oven to 190°C/375°F/ Gas 3. Grease a baking sheet. Cream the sugar, margarine and lemon rind together. Work in the flour and knead until smooth.

2 Roll out thinly and cut into rounds, then place on the baking sheet. Press on pieces of pineapple and bake for 15–20 minutes. Cool. Sandwich together with peanut butter, dust with icing sugar.

Ginger Cookies

If your children enjoy cooking with you, mixing and rolling the dough, or cutting out different shapes, this is the ideal recipe to let them practise on.

Makes 16

INGREDIENTS

115g/4oz/⅔ cup soft brown sugar
115g/4oz/½ cup soft margarine
pinch of salt
few drops of vanilla essence
175g/6oz/1¼ cups wholemeal plain flour
15g/½oz/1 tbsp cocoa, sifted
10ml/2 tsp ground ginger
a little milk
glacé icing and glacé cherries, to decorate

1 Preheat the oven to 190°C/375°F/ Gas 5. Grease a baking sheet. Cream together the sugar, margarine, salt and vanilla essence until very soft and light.

2 Work in the flour, cocoa and ginger, adding a little milk, if necessary, to bind the mixture. Knead lightly on a floured surface until smooth.

3 Roll out the dough to about 5mm/¼in thick. Stamp out shapes using floured biscuit cutters and place on the prepared baking sheet.

4 Bake the cookies for 10–15 minutes. Leave to cool on the baking sheets until firm, then transfer to a wire rack to cool completely. Decorate with glacé icing and pieces of glacé cherries.

Gingerbread Jungle

Snappy biscuits in animal shapes, which can be decorated in your own style.

Makes 14

INGREDIENTS

175g/6oz/1½ cups self-raising flour
2.5ml/½ tsp bicarbonate of soda
2.5ml/½ tsp ground cinnamon
10ml/2 tsp caster sugar
50g/2oz/¼ cup butter
45ml/3 tbsp golden syrup
50g/2oz/½ cup icing sugar
5–10ml/1–2 tsp water

Cook's Tip Any cutters can be used with the same mixture. Obviously, the smaller the cutters, the more biscuits you will make.

1 Preheat the oven to 190°C/375°F/Gas 5. Lightly oil two baking sheets.

2 Put the flour, bicarbonate of soda, cinnamon and caster sugar in a bowl and mix together. Melt the butter and syrup in a saucepan. Pour over the dry ingredients.

3 Mix together well and then use your hands to pull the mixture together to make a dough.

4 Turn on to a lightly floured surface and roll out to about 5mm/¼in thick.

5 Use floured animal cutters to cut shapes from the dough and arrange on the prepared baking sheets, leaving enough room between them to rise.

6 Press the trimmings back into a ball, roll it out and cut more shapes. Continue until all the dough is used. Bake for 8–12 minutes, until lightly browned.

7 Leave to cool slightly, before transferring to a wire rack with a palette knife. Sift the icing sugar into a small bowl and add enough water to make a fairly soft icing.

8 Spoon the icing into a piping bag fitted with a small, plain nozzle and pipe decorations on the cookies.

Sweet Necklaces

These are too fiddly for young children to make but ideal as novelty Christmas presents. Arrange in a pretty, tissue-lined box or tin for presentation.

Makes 12

INGREDIENTS

1 quantity Lebkuchen mixture
200g/7oz royal icing
pink food colouring
selection of small sweets
6m/6 yards fine pink, blue or white ribbon

1 Preheat the oven to 180°C/350°F/Gas 4. Grease two large baking sheets. Roll out slightly more than half of the Lebkuchen mixture on a lightly floured surface to a thickness of 5mm/¼in.

2 Cut out stars using a floured 2.5cm/1in star cutter. Transfer to a baking sheet, spacing them evenly. Taking care not to distort the shape of the stars, make a large hole in the centre of each, using a metal or wooden skewer.

3 Gather the trimmings together with the remaining dough. Roll the dough under the palms of your hands, to make a thick sausage about 2.5cm/1in in diameter. Cut in 1cm/½in slices. Using the skewer, make a hole in the centre of each. Put on the second baking sheet.

4 Bake for about 8 minutes, until slightly risen and just beginning to colour. Remove from the oven and, while still warm, re-make the skewer holes as the gingerbread will have spread slightly during baking. Leave to cool on a wire rack.

5 Put half the royal icing in a paper piping bag and snip off a tip. Use to pipe outlines around the stars. Colour the remaining icing with the pink colouring. Spoon into a paper piping bag fitted with a star nozzle.

6 Cut the sweets into smaller pieces and use to decorate the biscuits. Leave to harden.

7 Cut the ribbon into 50cm/20in lengths. Thread a selection of the biscuits on to each ribbon.

Choc-tipped Cookies

Get those cold hands wrapped round a steaming hot drink, and tuck into choc-tipped cookies.

Makes 22

INGREDIENTS

115g/4oz/½ cup margarine
45ml/3 tbsp icing sugar, sifted
150g/5oz/1¼ cups plain flour
few drops vanilla essence
75g/3oz plain chocolate, chopped

1 Preheat the oven to 180°C/350°F/ Gas 4. Lightly grease two baking sheets. Put the margarine and icing sugar in a bowl and cream them together until very soft. Mix in the flour and vanilla essence.

2 Spoon the mixture into a large piping bag fitted with a large star nozzle and pipe 10–13cm/4–5in lines on the prepared baking sheets. Cook for 15–20 minutes, until pale golden brown. Leave to cool slightly before lifting on to a wire rack. Leave the biscuits to cool completely.

3 Put the chocolate in a small heatproof bowl. Stand in a saucepan of hot, but not boiling, water and leave to melt. Dip both ends of each biscuit into the chocolate, put back on the rack and leave to set. Serve with hot chocolate topped with whipped cream.

Cook's Tip Make round biscuits if you prefer, and dip half of each biscuit in the melted chocolate.

Five-spice Fingers

Light, crumbly biscuits with an unusual Chinese five-spice flavouring.

Makes 28

INGREDIENTS

115g/4oz/$^{1}/_{2}$ cup margarine
50g/2oz/$^{1}/_{2}$ cup icing sugar
115g/4oz/1 cup plain flour
10ml/2 tsp five-spice powder
grated rind and juice of $^{1}/_{2}$ orange

1 Preheat the oven to 180°C/350°F/Gas 4. Lightly grease two baking sheets. Put the margarine and half the icing sugar in a bowl and beat with a wooden spoon, until the mixture is smooth and creamy.

2 Add the flour and five-spice powder and beat again. Spoon the mixture into a large piping bag fitted with a large star nozzle.

3 Pipe short lines of mixture, about 7.5cm/3in long, on the prepared baking sheets. Leave enough room for them to spread.

4 Bake for 15 minutes, until lightly browned. Leave to cool slightly, before transferring to a wire rack with a palette knife.

5 Sift the remaining icing sugar into a small bowl and stir in the orange rind. Add enough juice to make a thin icing. Brush over the biscuits while they are still warm.

Cook's Tip These biscuits are delicious served with ice cream or creamy desserts.

Gingerbread Teddies

These endearing teddies, dressed in striped pyjamas, would make a perfect gift for friends of any age. If you can't get a large cutter, make smaller teddies or use a traditional gingerbread-man cutter. You might need some help from an adult for the decorating.

Makes 6

INGREDIENTS

75g/3oz white chocolate, chopped
175g/6oz ready-to-roll white sugar paste
blue food colouring
25g/1oz plain or milk chocolate
For the gingerbread
175g/6oz/1½ cups plain flour
1.5ml/¼ tsp bicarbonate of soda
pinch of salt
5ml/1 tsp ground ginger
5ml/1 tsp ground cinnamon
65g/2½oz/⅓ cup unsalted butter, chopped
75g/3oz/⅓ cup caster sugar
30ml/2 tbsp maple or golden syrup
1 egg yolk, beaten

1 To make the gingerbread, sift together the flour, bicarbonate of soda, salt and spices into a large bowl. Rub the butter into the flour until the mixture resembles fine breadcrumbs.

2 Stir in the sugar, syrup and egg yolk and mix to a firm dough. Knead lightly. Wrap and chill for 30 minutes.

3 Preheat the oven to 180°C/350°F/Gas 4. Grease two large baking sheets. Roll out the gingerbread dough on a floured surface and cut out teddies, using a floured 13cm/5in cookie cutter.

4 Transfer to the prepared baking sheets and bake for 10–15 minutes, until just beginning to colour around the edges. Leave on the baking sheets for 3 minutes and then transfer to a wire rack.

5 Melt half of the white chocolate. Put in a paper piping bag and snip off the tip. Make a neat template for the teddies' clothes: draw an outline of the cutter on to paper, finishing at the neck, halfway down the arms and around the legs.

6 Thinly roll the sugar paste on a surface dusted with icing sugar. Use the template to cut out the clothes, and secure them to the biscuits with the melted chocolate.

7 Use the sugar paste trimmings to add ears, eyes and snouts. Dilute the blue colouring with a little water and use it to paint the striped pyjamas.

8 Melt the remaining white chocolate and the plain or milk chocolate in separate bowls over saucepans of hot water. Put in separate paper piping bags and snip off the tips. Use the white chocolate to pipe a decorative outline around the pyjamas and use the plain or milk chocolate to pipe the faces.

Cookie Treats and Gifts

Everyone has times when they feel the need to indulge themselves. If your fancy is for something rich and sweet, or if you want to give someone a treat, delve into the next few pages and you will find just the ticket.

A delicious gift that is home-made is always received with delight, and cookies, because they have a special place in nearly everyone's heart, are doubly acceptable, even if they are simple. Of course, if the cookies require a little extra skill, such as Honey and Nut Clusters, they will be received with even more pleasure. With home-made cookies, it is so easy to hit upon an ideal gift every time, whether it is just a small token or something very special.

The slightly more complicated cookies are also particularly therapeutic to make and provide a rewarding job for a quiet morning or afternoon, or a rainy day when you want to bring a little sunshine into your life. However, none of the recipes in this chapter is beyond the bounds of a reasonably competent home cook.

Chocolate Nut Clusters

These are an ideal way to end a dinner party, or a gift for a special friend.

Makes 30

INGREDIENTS

550ml/18fl oz/2¼ cups double cream
25g/1oz/2 tbsp unsalted butter, chopped
350ml/12fl oz/1½ cups golden syrup
200g/7oz/scant 1 cup granulated sugar
90g/3½oz/½ packed cup light brown sugar
pinch of salt
15ml/1 tbsp vanilla essence
425g/15oz/3¾ cups hazelnuts, pecans, walnuts, brazil nuts or unsalted peanuts, or a combination
400g/14oz plain chocolate, chopped
25g/1oz/2 tbsp white vegetable fat

1 Lightly oil two baking sheets. In a heavy-based saucepan over a medium heat, cook the first six ingredients until the sugars dissolve and the butter melts. Bring to the boil and cook, stirring frequently, for about 1 hour, until the caramel reaches 119°C/238°F (soft ball stage) on a sugar thermometer.

2 Place the bottom of the saucepan in a pan of cold water to stop cooking, or transfer the caramel to a smaller saucepan. Cool slightly, then stir in the vanilla essence.

3 Stir the nuts into the caramel until well-coated. Using an oiled tablespoon, drop spoonfuls of the nut mixture on to the prepared sheets, about 2.5cm/1in apart. If the mixture hardens, return to the heat to soften.

4 Refrigerate the clusters for 30 minutes, until firm and cold, or leave in a cool place until hardened.

Cook's Tip If you do not possess a sugar thermometer, you can test cooked sugar for 'soft ball stage' by spooning a small amount into a bowl of cold water: when taken out it should form a soft ball when rolled between finger and thumb.

5 Using a metal palette knife, transfer the clusters to a wire rack placed over a baking sheet to catch drips.

6 In a medium saucepan, over a low heat, melt the chocolate and white vegetable fat, stirring until smooth. Cool slightly.

7 Spoon chocolate over each cluster, being sure to cover completely. Alternatively, using a fork, dip each cluster into chocolate and lift out, tapping on the edge of the saucepan to shake off excess.

8 Place on the wire rack over the baking sheet. Allow to set for 2 hours, until hardened.

Louisiana Pralines

This version of pralines resembles puddles of nut fudge and is deliciously indulgent.

Makes 30

INGREDIENTS

225g/8oz/2 cups pecan halves
450g/1lb/2 well-packed cups soft light brown sugar
200g/7oz/scant 1 cup granulated sugar
300ml/½ pint/1¼ cups double cream
175ml/6fl oz/¾ cup milk
5ml/1 tsp vanilla essence

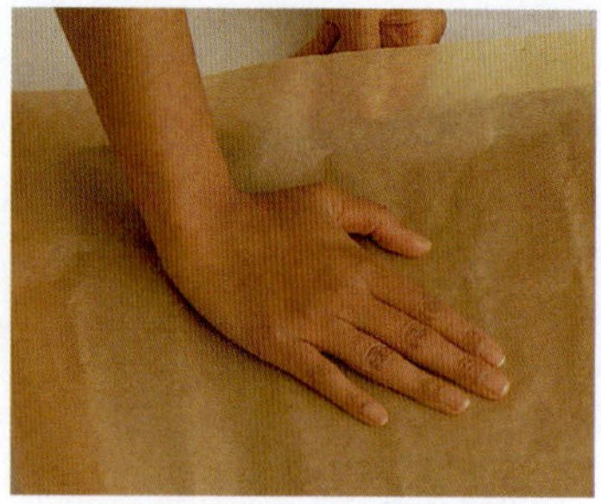

1 Roughly chop half of the pecans and set all the nuts aside. Line 2–3 baking sheets with non-stick baking paper.

2 Stir both sugars, the cream and milk together in a heavy-based saucepan over a medium heat. Stir until the mixture reaches 119°C/238°F or the soft ball stage.

3 Remove from the heat immediately and beat with an electric beater or balloon whisk until the mixture loses its sheen and becomes creamy in texture and grainy looking. This could take 15 minutes by hand or about 5 minutes with an electric beater.

4 Stir in the vanilla essence and nuts. Drop tablespoons of the mixture on to the prepared baking sheets, allowing it to spread of its own accord. Leave to cool and set at room temperature. Store between layers of greaseproof paper in an airtight container.

Chocolate-coated Nut Brittle

Equal amounts of pecans and almonds set in crisp caramel, then coated in dark chocolate, make a sensational gift.

Makes 20–24

INGREDIENTS

115g/4oz/1 cup mixed pecans and whole almonds
115g/4oz/½ cup caster sugar
60ml/4 tbsp water
200g/7oz plain chocolate, chopped

Cook's Tip These look best in rough chunks, so don't worry if the pieces break unevenly, or if there are gaps in the chocolate coating.

1 Lightly grease a baking sheet. Mix the nuts, sugar and water in a heavy-based saucepan. Place the pan over a low heat, stirring without boiling until the sugar has dissolved.

2 Bring to the boil, then lower the heat to medium and cook until the mixture turns a rich golden brown and registers 148°C/300°F on a sugar thermometer.

3 To test without a thermometer, drop a small amount of the mixture into a cup of iced water. The mixture should become brittle enough to snap with your fingers.

4 Quickly remove the pan from the heat and tip the mixture on to the prepared baking sheet, spreading it evenly. Leave until completely cold and hard.

5 Break the nut brittle into bite-size pieces. Melt the chocolate in a heatproof bowl over a saucepan of hot water and dip the pieces to half-coat them. Leave on a sheet of non-stick baking paper to set.

Chocolate Fudge Triangles

This fudge can be stored in an airtight container in the fridge for up to 2 weeks.

Makes 48

INGREDIENTS

600g/1lb 5oz fine quality white chocolate, chopped
400ml/14fl oz can sweetened condensed milk
15ml/1 tbsp vanilla essence
7.5ml/1½ tsp lemon juice
pinch of salt
215g/7½oz/scant 2 cups hazelnuts or pecans, chopped (optional)
175g/6oz plain chocolate, chopped
40g/1½oz/3 tbsp unsalted butter, chopped
50g/2oz plain chocolate, melted, to decorate

1 Line a 20cm/8in square baking tin with foil. In a saucepan over a low heat, melt the chocolate and condensed milk, stirring frequently. Remove from the heat and stir in the vanilla essence, lemon juice, salt, and nuts, if using. Spread half of the mixture in the tin. Chill for 15 minutes.

2 In a saucepan over a low heat, melt the plain chocolate and butter, stirring until smooth. Remove from the heat, cool slightly, then pour over the chilled white layer and chill for 15 minutes.

3 Gently re-heat the remaining white chocolate mixture and pour over the set plain chocolate layer. Smooth the top, then chill for 2–4 hours, until set.

4 Using the foil to lift it, remove the fudge from the tin and turn on to a cutting board. Remove the foil and, using a sharp knife, cut into 24 squares. Cut each square into two triangles. To decorate, drizzle with melted chocolate.

Honey and Nut Clusters

These are popular in Italy. To serve, cut in squares or fingers and keep in the refrigerator. They are delightfully sticky!

Makes 48

INGREDIENTS

115g/4oz/$^2/_3$ cup blanched almonds
115g/4oz/1 cup shelled hazelnuts
whites of 2 eggs
115g/4oz/$^1/_3$ cup clear honey
115g/4oz/$^1/_2$ cup caster sugar

1 Preheat the oven to the lowest temperature. Line a 20cm/8in square tin with baking paper.

2 Spread the almonds and hazelnuts on separate baking sheets and toast in the oven for about 30 minutes. Tip on to a cloth and rub off the skins. Roughly chop both types of nut.

3 Whisk the egg whites until they are stiff, and stir in the chopped nuts.

4 Put the honey and sugar into a small, heavy-based saucepan and bring to the boil. Stir in the nut mixture and cook over a medium heat for 10 minutes.

5 Turn the mixture into the prepared tin and level the top. Cover with another piece of non-stick paper, put weights (such as food cans) on top and chill for at least 2 days.

6 To present as a tree decoration, wrap slices in non-stick baking paper and then in gift-wrap or cotton fabric, or in foil.

Peppermint and Coconut Chocolate Sticks

Desiccated coconut gives these chocolate mint sticks a unique flavour and texture.

Makes 80

INGREDIENTS

115g/4oz/1/2 cup granulated sugar
150ml/1/4 pint/2/3 cup water
2.5ml/1/2 tsp peppermint essence
200g/7oz plain dark chocolate, chopped
60ml/4 tbsp toasted desiccated coconut

1 Lightly oil a large baking sheet. Place the sugar and water in a small, heavy-based saucepan and heat gently, stirring occasionally, until the sugar has dissolved completely.

2 Bring to the boil and boil rapidly without stirring until the syrup registers 138°C/280°F on a sugar thermometer. Remove the pan from the heat and add the peppermint essence, then pour on to the prepared baking sheet and leave until set and completely cold.

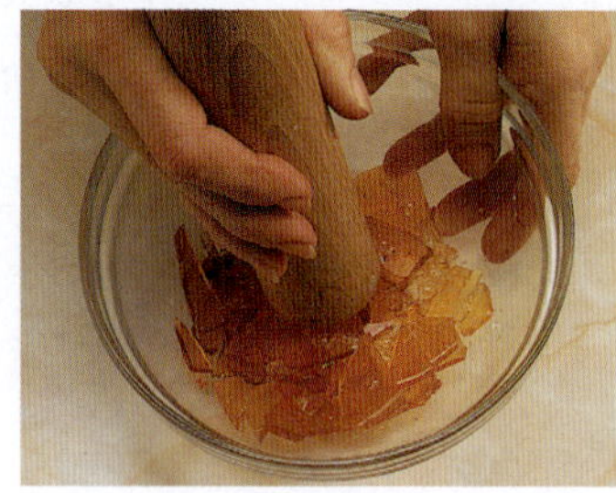

3 Break up the peppermint mixture into a bowl and use the end of a rolling pin to crush it into pieces.

4 Melt the chocolate in a heatproof bowl over a saucepan of hot water. Remove from the heat and stir in the mint pieces and desiccated coconut.

5 Place a 30 x 25cm/12 x 10in sheet of non-stick baking paper on a flat surface. Spread the mixture over the paper, leaving a narrow border all around. Leave to set. When firm, use a sharp knife to cut into thin sticks.

Chocolate Peppermint Crisps

If you do not have a sugar thermometer, test cooked sugar for "hard ball stage" by spooning a few drops into a bowl of cold water; it should form a hard ball when rolled between fingers.

Makes 30

INGREDIENTS

50g/2oz/¼ cup granulated sugar
50ml/2fl oz/¼ cup water
5ml/1 tsp peppermint essence
225g/8oz plain chocolate, chopped

1 Lightly brush a large baking sheet with unflavoured oil. In a saucepan over a medium heat, heat the sugar and water, swirling the pan gently until the sugar dissolves. Boil rapidly to 138°C/280°F on a sugar thermometer. Remove the pan from the heat and add the peppermint essence; swirl to mix. Pour on to the prepared baking sheet and leave to set and cool completely.

2 When cold, break into pieces. Place in a food processor fitted with a metal blade and process to fine crumbs form; do not over-process.

3 Line two baking sheets with non-stick baking paper. Place the chocolate in a small heatproof bowl over a small saucepan of hot water. Place over a very low heat until the chocolate has melted, stirring frequently until smooth. Remove from the heat and stir in the peppermint mixture.

4 Using a teaspoon, drop small mounds on to the prepared sheets. Using the back of the spoon, spread to 4cm/1½in rounds. Cool, then refrigerate for about 1 hour, until set. Peel off the paper and store in airtight containers with non-stick baking paper between the layers.

Striped Biscuits

These biscuits may be made in different flavours and colours and look wonderful tied in bundles or packed into boxes. Eat them with ice cream or light desserts.

Makes 25

INGREDIENTS

25g/1oz white chocolate, melted
red and green food colouring dusts
2 egg whites
90g/3½oz/⅓ cup caster sugar
50g/2oz/½ cup plain flour
50g/2oz/4 tbsp unsalted butter, melted

1 Preheat the oven to 190°C/375°F/Gas 5. Line two baking sheets with non-stick baking paper. Divide the melted chocolate in half and add a little food colouring dust to each half to colour the chocolate red and green. Using two greaseproof paper piping bags, fill with each colour chocolate and fold down the tops. Snip off the points.

2 Place the egg whites in a bowl and whisk until stiff. Add the sugar gradually, whisking well after each addition, to make a thick meringue. Add the flour and melted butter and whisk until smooth.

3 Drop four separate teaspoonfuls of the mixture on to the prepared baking sheets and spread into thin rounds. Pipe lines or zigzags of green and red chocolate over each round.

4 Bake one sheet at a time for 3–4 minutes, until pale golden in colour. Loosen the rounds with a palette knife and return to the oven for a few seconds to soften. Have two or three lightly oiled wooden spoon handles at hand.

5 Taking one round biscuit out of the oven at a time, roll it around a spoon handle and leave for a few seconds to set. Repeat to shape the remaining biscuits. Put the second sheet of biscuits in to bake.

6 When the biscuits are set, slip them off the spoon handles on to a wire rack. Repeat with the remaining mixture and the red and green chocolate until all the mixture has been used, baking only one sheet of biscuits at a time. If the biscuits are too hard to shape, simply return them to the oven for a few seconds to soften.

7 When the biscuits are cold, tie them together with coloured ribbon and pack into boxes, tins or glass jars.

Almond Fingers

A very simple Middle Eastern sweetmeat which is especially popular in Arab countries.

Makes 40–50

INGREDIENTS

200g/7oz/1$\frac{3}{4}$ cups ground almonds
50g/2oz/$\frac{1}{2}$ cup ground pistachios
50g/2oz/$\frac{1}{4}$ cup granulated sugar
15ml/1 tbsp rosewater
2.5ml/$\frac{1}{2}$ tsp ground cinnamon
12 sheets of filo pastry
115g/4oz/$\frac{1}{2}$ cup butter, melted
icing sugar for dusting

1 Preheat the oven to 160°C/325°F/ Gas 3. Butter a baking sheet. Mix together the almonds, pistachios, sugar, rosewater and cinnamon.

2 Cut each sheet of filo pastry into four rectangles. Work with one at a time, and cover the remaining rectangles with a damp dish towel.

3 Brush one rectangle with melted butter, place a teaspoon of the nut filling in the centre.

4 Fold the sides and roll into a cigar shape. Continue until all the filling has been used.

5 Place the 'cigars' on the baking sheet and bake for 30 minutes. Transfer to a wire rack to cool, then dust with icing sugar.

Basbousa

These delicious Middle Eastern coconut sweetmeats can be served either hot as a dessert or cold with tea.

Makes 12

INGREDIENTS

115g/4oz/$\frac{1}{2}$ cup unsalted butter
175g/6oz/$\frac{3}{4}$ cup caster sugar
50g/2oz/$\frac{1}{2}$ cup plain flour
150g/5oz/1$\frac{1}{4}$ cups semolina
75g/3oz/1$\frac{1}{2}$ cups grated coconut
175ml/6fl oz/$\frac{3}{4}$ cup milk
5ml/1 tsp baking powder
5ml/1 tsp vanilla essence
almonds, to decorate
For the syrup
115g/4oz/$\frac{1}{2}$ cup caster sugar
150ml/$\frac{1}{4}$ pint/$\frac{2}{3}$ cup water
15ml/1 tbsp lemon juice

1 To make the syrup, place the sugar, water and lemon juice in a saucepan, bring to the boil, simmer for 6–8 minutes then cool before chilling.

2 Preheat the oven to 180°C/350°F/ Gas 4. Melt the butter in a saucepan. Add the remaining ingredients and mix thoroughly.

3 Pour the cake mixture into a shallow baking tin, flatten the top and bake for 30–35 minutes.

4 Remove the Basbousa from the oven and cut into diamond-shaped lozenges. Pour the cold syrup evenly over the top and decorate with an almond placed in each centre.

Semolina and Nut Halva

Semolina is a popular ingredient in many desserts and pastries in the Eastern Mediterranean. Here it provides a spongy base for soaking up a deliciously fragrant spicy syrup.

Makes 20–24

INGREDIENTS

115g/4oz/½ cup unsalted butter
115g/4oz/½ cup caster sugar
finely grated rind of 1 orange
30ml/2 tbsp orange juice
3 eggs
175g/6oz/1 cup semolina
10ml/2 tsp baking powder
115g/4oz/1 cup ground hazelnuts
50g/2oz/½ cup unblanched hazelnuts, toasted and chopped
50g/2oz/½ cup blanched almonds, toasted and chopped
shredded rind of 1 orange
For the syrup
350g/12oz/1½ cups caster sugar
550ml/18fl oz/2¼ cups water
2 cinnamon sticks, halved
juice of 1 lemon
60ml/4 tbsp orange flower water

1 Preheat the oven to 220°C/425°F/Gas 7. Grease and line the base of a deep 23cm/9in square heavy-based cake tin.

2 Lightly cream the butter in a bowl. Add the sugar, orange rind and juice, the eggs, semolina, baking powder and hazelnuts and beat the ingredients together until smooth.

3 Turn into the prepared tin and level the surface. Bake for 20–25 minutes, until just firm and golden. Leave to cool in the tin.

4 To make the syrup, put the sugar in a heavy-based saucepan with the water and cinnamon sticks. Heat gently, until the sugar has dissolved.

5 Bring to the boil and boil hard for 5 minutes. Measure half the syrup in a jug and add the lemon juice and orange flower water to it. Pour over the halva. Reserve the remainder of the syrup in the pan.

6 Leave the halva in the tin until the syrup is absorbed, then turn it out on to a plate and cut diagonally into diamond-shaped portions. Scatter with the nuts.

7 Boil the remaining syrup until slightly thickened then pour it over the halva. Scatter the shredded orange rind over the cake and serve with lightly whipped cream.

Jewelled Elephants

These stunningly robed elephants make a lovely gift for animal-lovers, or an edible decoration for a special occasion. If you make holes in them before baking, you could use them as original Christmas tree decorations.

Makes 10

INGREDIENTS

1 quantity Lebkuchen mixture
1 quantity Icing Glaze
red food colouring
225g/8oz ready-to-roll sugar paste
small candy-covered chocolates or chews
gold dragees

1 Preheat the oven to 180°C/350°F/Gas 4. Grease two large baking sheets. Make a paper template for the elephant. Roll out the Lebkuchen mixture. Use the template and a sharp knife to cut out elephant shapes. Space them, slightly apart, on the baking sheet for 3 minutes and then transfer to a wire rack to cool.

2 Put a little Icing Glaze in a paper piping bag fitted with a fine nozzle. Alternatively, cut off the tip of the bag.

3 Knead some red food colouring into half of the sugar paste. Roll a little red sugar paste under your fingers into ropes. Secure them around the feet and tips of the trunk, using icing from the bag. Shape more red sugar paste into flat oval shapes, about 2cm/¾in long, and stick them to the elephants' heads. Shape smaller ovals and secure them at the top of the trunks.

4 Roll out the white sugar paste. Cut out circles, using a 6cm/2½in biscuit cutter. Secure to the elephants' backs with royal icing so that the edge of the sugar paste is about 2.5cm/1in above the top of the legs. Trim off the excess paste around the top of the white sugar paste shapes.

5 Pipe 1cm/½in tassels around the edges. Pipe dots of white icing at the tops of the trunks, around the necks and at the tops of the tails and also use it to draw small eyes. Halve the small sweets and press the halves into the sugar paste, above the tassels. Decorate the headdress, sweets and white sugar paste with gold dragees, securing them with dots of icing. Leave for several hours, to harden.

Index

Notes

Notes

Notes

NOTES

Notes

Notes

Notes

Notes